fondue ON THE MENU

Edited by BEVERLY KEES and DONNIE FLORA

Photographer: FRED SCHULZE
Illustrator: BARBARA BASCOVE

GOLDEN PRESS 🦅 **NEW YORK**
WESTERN PUBLISHING COMPANY, INC.
RACINE, WISCONSIN

Art Director
REMO COSENTINO

Designer
DIANNA ROLFSEN

CONTENTS

Introduction

Fondue! What began as a simple Swiss peasant meal born of necessity progressed to become a trademark of Swiss cuisine; today, it occupies a prominent place in the entertaining plans of American hostesses.

What led to this phenomenal popularity? Why does the fondue pot now threaten to displace the chafing dish for at-home entertaining this side of the Atlantic?

Well—the fondue party is easy; it's convivial; it's different; and it allows the hostess to be a partygoer, too.

Clearly, none of these is a conclusive reason, but it hardly matters—what is clear is that fondue is here to stay. More interesting than reasons, perhaps, is a bit of the background of fondue.

The word "fondue" derives from the French verb *fondre*—to melt. And legend has it that fondue was originated by a Swiss shepherd weary of his monotonous winter fare of hard bread, cheese and wine. Perhaps it was by accident that he lit a fire under his iron pot, tossed in the cheese, added some wine and dipped the bread into the bubbling cheese mixture. If so, it was a happy accident. The idea spread and was eventually seized upon by the hospitable Swiss innkeepers.

There it remained for some time—a national dish to be enjoyed in Switzerland or a dish prepared in this country by a professional chef at a restaurant featuring international cuisine.

How the current trend toward fondue cooking in America started no one knows for certain. What is certain is that almost overnight fondue pots began popping up in window displays, in housewares departments, in mail order catalogs. This proliferation offers convincing proof that fondue has become very much a part of the American scene.

Without a fondue pot, you can't have a fondue party. Therefore, a word about choosing one.

Your best and most versatile investment is a good quality metal pot—this is the only material which will withstand the heat required to cook meat fondues as well as produce excellent cheese and dessert fondues over low heat.

5

Introduction

On the other hand, if you plan to make just cheese or dessert fondues (or both), a good quality earthenware pot will perform consistently and well. Please, though—don't ever try cooking a meat fondue in a earthenware pot. The pot is almost certain to crack under the high heat and the results could be disastrous. Earthenware was never intended to withstand the high temperature needed for meat fondues.

You have an earthenware pot; your cheese fondues are always a smash and you're thinking of trying a meat fondue for a change? Great! But before you rush out and buy a special pot, try a beef fondue in your electric skillet. Get your family's opinion and then decide whether a new pot is a smart investment.

A second word, this one about burners. An electrically controlled burner will insure a constant, even temperature—exact and steady. It is relatively expensive, but well worth the cost if you are a dedicated fondue-r. Burners that are fired by denatured alcohol, butane gas or Sterno are less expensive than electric burners, but the heat they generate is harder to control at an even temperature. And temperature can be the difference between the success and failure of your fondue. If budget rules your choice, be sure to keep an eye on the flame.

Long-handled fondue forks are a must for fondue parties; compartmented plates aren't necessary but are a nice addition (they keep sauces from running together) and are readily available.

In the chapters that follow, you'll find recipes for all kinds of fondues. Most main dish fondues are accompanied by complete menus—delectable dishes (with recipes) that are perfect complements to the fondue. Meat and seafood fondues carry suggestions for a full array of sauces—and recipes for them. We've even included special marinades to give an extra tang.

Many menus are keyed to international themes—a bonanza for the hostess who revels in entertaining with flair right down to the background music and appropriate decor.

There are out-of-the-ordinary fondues to impress the fondue lover who thinks he has tasted them all. There are dessert fondues that will give you a new slant on how to leave your guests asking —or at least wishing they could—"When's the *next* party?"

Now about wines—for no fondue party is complete without them. They add that extra something that "makes" the party. They're a perfect accompaniment to the meal itself and the ideal aperitif. Cocktails take a back seat at cheese fondue parties. And water isn't served at all; it simply doesn't sit well with melted cheese.

Select the wines for your home fondue parties carefully. It's not hard to develop your own expertise on the subject. And wines needn't be expensive. There are excellent domestic varieties available at modest prices. The important thing is to know the right type of wine to serve with each fondue.

We've given you suggestions with the menus but here are some general basic tenets you may find helpful. Serve light and dry wines before and during the meal, sweet wines with dessert. White wines are served before red—and with fish or fowl. Red wines enhance the flavor of red meats and cheese. Use a full-bodied wine for strong-flavored fondue sauces, a delicately flavored wine for subtle sauces. Rosé goes with any type of food.

Wines should be stored racked, lying on their sides. One exception: red wines should be allowed to stand upright overnight and the cork removed one hour before serving. This will allow the sediment which tends to accumulate in red wines to drop to the bottom of the bottle, leaving the wine clear.

To serve, bring still red wines to room temperature (white wines are served chilled), then slit and remove the foil cap. Remove any mold from around the cork with a damp cloth; uncork and wipe the inside of the bottle lip before decanting. Proper wine service also requires that the host sample the wine first to be sure that it has not picked up the flavor of the cork.

There you are—all set to entertain at your first or your 101st fondue party. Fire up the pot, light the candles and pour the wine. Ahead of you lies a memorable evening of good food and good conversation with good friends.

Cheese Fondues

Let's begin the way the Swiss did—with cheese fondue, and its many variations. Many cheeses melt well and thus lend themselves to fondue. Our Cheese Chart (pages 30 and 31) gives a quick rundown on these as well as on other cheeses which are included in menus throughout the book. Use the chart, too, if one of these recipes calls for a cheese with which you are not familiar—or if you have to substitute because a particular cheese isn't available.

What else can you expect to find in this chapter? Menus featuring cheese fondues in profusion—the Classic Swiss, of course, but also a Green Cheese Fondue, Cheddar-Beer, Gorgonzola-Tilsiter, Potato-Cheese, Horseradish, Tomato and Blue Cheese Fondues. Even if you're familiar with cheese fondue, we think you'll find many of these exciting surprises!

A few mild words of advice may be in order here—by way of either prevention or cure—if something should go awry with your cheese fondue. Do use a light dry wine (such as Rhine, Riesling, Chablis or Neuchâtel) in the fondue; if you must substitute a slightly sweeter wine, add one or two teaspoons of lemon juice. Keep the flame under the fondue low. If your fondue should turn lumpy, stringy or too thick, return it to the kitchen range and stir with a wire whisk while adding ½ teaspoon cornstarch blended with a little wine. Back to normal!

For dunking into the fondue? Cubes of sourdough French bread are the classic choice; but try raw vegetables and cubes of cooked meat or seafood for a change of pace.

You might include this fondue "tradition" as part of your party: If a man loses his bread cube in the cheese during dunking, he can choose a girl to kiss. If a girl loses her bread cube—she has to kiss *all* the men!

And don't forget that delectable brown crust that forms at the bottom of any cheese fondue pot. Loosen it with a knife and divide it evenly among the guests. It's a real delicacy!

Classic Swiss Fondue
Menu

Classic Swiss Fondue
Parsleyed Potatoes
Belgian Endive Salad
with French Dressing
Mocha Ricotta
Dry Swiss Neuchâtel

4 to 6 servings

CLASSIC SWISS FONDUE

1 clove garlic, halved	3 tbsp. flour
2 cups very dry white wine	¼ cup kirsch
1 lb. coarsely grated Gruyère or	Nutmeg (optional)
Emmenthaler cheese or ½ lb.	Salt and pepper (optional)
each	Cubes of sourdough French
	bread

Rub inside of the fondue pot with garlic; discard garlic. Heat the wine in the pot until almost boiling. Add the cheese, dredged in flour, by handfuls, making sure each addition has melted and blended before adding more. When all the cheese has been added and the mixture is smooth and thick, stir in the kirsch; add nutmeg, salt and pepper. Serve with the bread cubes for dunking.

Note: For the mildest fondue, use all Emmenthaler (Swiss) cheese. The strongest fondue is made from well-aged Gruyère. Try half and half for a medium flavor variation.

PARSLEYED POTATOES

1½ lbs. (12 to 16) small, peeled potatoes	4 tbsp. butter
	1 tbsp. minced parsley

Boil potatoes. When done, drain and toss lightly with butter and parsley.

BELGIAN ENDIVE SALAD WITH FRENCH DRESSING

6 Belgian endive	Chopped fresh parsley
French Dressing (see page 13)	

Cut endive stalks in half lengthwise. Wash in cold water and separate all of the leaves. Dry thoroughly on paper towels. Toss endive with French Dressing in a salad bowl until well coated. Sprinkle with parsley.

MOCHA RICOTTA

1 lb. creamed ricotta cheese
½ cup grated semisweet chocolate
  Sugar to taste (optional)

2 tbsp. crème de café
3 to 4 tbsp. heavy cream
  Chopped salted peanuts
  (optional)

Cream together the cheese and chocolate. Taste; beat in sugar, then the liqueur. Add enough of the cream to make a smooth consistency; add a little more sugar if desired. Pour into sherbet or parfait glasses and chill well. Serve garnished with chopped peanuts, if desired.

CARAWAY CHEESE FONDUE
MENU

Caraway Cheese Fondue
Tossed Salad with
Sour Cream-Dill Dressing
Fresh Fruit Dessert
Aquavit and Beer

4 to 6 servings

CARAWAY CHEESE FONDUE

1 clove garlic
2 cups dry Sauterne
1 lb. Emmenthaler cheese,
    coarsely grated
3 tbsp. flour

¼ cup rum
½ cup caraway seeds
Salt and pepper to taste
Cubes of rye and French breads

Rub inside of the fondue pot with garlic; discard garlic. Heat the wine in the pot until almost boiling. Add the cheese, dredged in flour, by handfuls, making sure each addition has melted and blended before adding more. When all the cheese has been added and the mixture is smooth and thick, stir in the rum; add caraway seeds, salt and pepper. Serve with the bread cubes for dunking.

SOUR CREAM-DILL DRESSING

1 cup dairy sour cream
1 tsp. grated onion or fresh
    onion juice

1 tsp. dill seed
½ tsp. salt
Dash white pepper

Beat sour cream until smooth. Add rest of ingredients and blend. Use over tossed salad.

FRESH FRUIT DESSERT

2 cups water
1⅓ cups sugar
2 tbsp. lemon juice
1 tsp. vanilla
2 oranges, sectioned
    (white removed)

2 pears, cut in eighths
1 cup fresh pineapple cubes
1 cup fresh peach or apricot
    cubes
1 cup fresh pitted cherries

Make a thin syrup by boiling the first three ingredients together for five minutes. Stir in vanilla. Let syrup cool to warm temperature; pour over the fruit.

Note: Syrup will not get thick, even after cooling; it is meant to be of a thin consistency.

Green Cheese Fondue Menu

GREEN CHEESE FONDUE

1 clove garlic, halved
2 cups very dry white wine
1 lb. coarsely grated Gruyère or Emmenthaler cheese or ½ lb. each
½ cup grated Sapsago cheese

2 tbsp. flour
¼ cup kirsch
Nutmeg (optional)
Salt and pepper (optional)
Cubes of sourdough French bread

Rub inside of the fondue pot with garlic; discard garlic. Heat the wine in the pot until almost boiling. Add the cheese, dredged in flour, by handfuls, making sure each addition has melted and blended before adding more. When all the cheese has been added and the mixture is smooth and thick, stir in the kirsch; add nutmeg, salt and pepper. Serve with the bread cubes for dunking.

Note: This is to celebrate going to the moon. (Sapsago is the green cheese the moon was supposedly made of.)

FRENCH DRESSING

1½ tsp. salt
½ tsp. paprika
¾ tsp. dry mustard

Dash cayenne pepper
⅓ cup wine vinegar
1 cup vegetable oil

Combine dry ingredients. Add vinegar and oil. Shake vigorously. Serve over halved cherry tomatoes on a bed of lettuce.

COFFEE GELATIN

2 envelopes (2 tbsp.) unflavored gelatin
½ cup coffee liqueur
3 cups coffee
¾ cup sugar

Pinch salt
Sweetened whipped cream, flavored with lemon extract
Lemon twists

In a bowl sprinkle gelatin over liqueur to soften. In a saucepan, warm the coffee and sugar together until the sugar is dissolved. Add the gelatin mixture and salt; stir and heat until all the gelatin is dissolved and the mixture is perfectly clear. Pour liquid into individual molds and chill several hours. Unmold; garnish with whipped cream and lemon twists.

Green Cheese Fondue
Cherry Tomatoes with French Dressing
Coffee Gelatin
Dry Swiss Neuchâtel

4 to 6 servings

13

CHAMPAGNE FONDUE
with Truffles
MENU

Champagne Fondue with Truffles
Caesar Salad
Crème Vert
Dry White Burgundy

4 to 6 servings

CHAMPAGNE FONDUE WITH TRUFFLES

2 canned truffles
2 cups brut champagne
1 lb. Emmenthaler cheese, coarsely grated

3 tbsp. flour
Nutmeg
Cubes of sourdough French bread

Drain truffles, reserving the liquid, and slice thinly. Heat truffles in fondue pot with champagne and truffle liquid until almost boiling. Add cheese, dredged in flour, by handfuls, making sure each addition melts before more is added. Add a grating of nutmeg after the last addition has melted and is blended thoroughly. Serve with the bread cubes for dunking.

CAESAR SALAD

1 clove garlic, sliced
½ cup olive oil
1 cup French bread cubes
2 heads romaine
1½ tsp. salt
¼ tsp. dry mustard
Freshly ground black pepper

5 anchovy fillets, mashed into a paste
3 tbsp. wine vinegar
1 egg
Juice of 1 lemon
2 to 3 tbsp. Parmesan cheese

Marinate garlic in oil several hours; discard garlic. Sauté the bread cubes in 2 tablespoons of the oil. In bowl, break up romaine into bite-size pieces. Sprinkle over it the salt, dry mustard, grating of black pepper and anchovies. Add vinegar and remaining oil. Crack the egg onto romaine. Squeeze the lemon juice over the egg. Add croutons and cheese and toss well. Serve at once.

CRÈME VERT

3 ripe avocados
6 tbsp. sugar

Juice of 1 lemon or 2 limes

Puree the avocado meat. Beat in half the sugar and all the citrus juice. Taste; correct sweetness by adding remaining sugar gradually. Pour into sherbet or parfait glasses and chill until very cold.

14

CHEDDAR-BEER FONDUE

1 clove garlic	½ tsp. dry mustard
1 lb. well-aged sharp Cheddar cheese	2 cups dry beer (good quality)
3 tbsp. flour	2 tbsp. chopped chives
1 tsp. Worcestershire sauce	Cubes of sourdough French bread

Rub inside of the fondue pot with garlic; discard garlic. Heat the beer in the pot until almost boiling. Add the cheese, dredged in flour, by handfuls, making sure each addition has melted and blended before adding more. When all the cheese has been added and the mixture is smooth and thick, stir in the Worcestershire sauce; add dry mustard. Garnish with chives. Serve with the bread cubes for dunking.

Note: For change-of-pace dunking, use pieces of cooked sausage or hot dogs, meatballs, pieces of waffle, canapé-size sandwiches or apple slices.

TOMATOES VINAIGRETTE

1 clove garlic, minced	⅔ cup olive oil
1 tsp. salt	6 large tomatoes, cut in half crosswise
½ tsp. pepper	Leaf lettuce
2 tsp. oregano	Green onions
½ tsp. dry mustard	Parsley
⅓ cup wine vinegar	

Combine first seven ingredients in a jar and shake vigorously; discard garlic. Pour over tomato halves or thick slices of tomato. Refrigerate at least two hours, basting occasionally. Serve on leaf lettuce; top with chopped green onion tops, parsley and more of the marinade.

Cheddar-Beer Fondue
Tomatoes Vinaigrette
Danish Applesauce Torte
Beer

4 to 6 servings

15

Cheddar-Beer Fondue
Menu

DANISH APPLESAUCE TORTE

1 lb. can (2 cups) thick, lightly sweetened applesauce
1⅓ cups finely ground blanched almonds

½ cup confectioners' sugar
3 eggs, separated
Whipped cream (optional)

Preheat oven to 350°. Butter a 1-quart baking dish and pour in the applesauce. Combine the almonds with the sugar; beat in the egg yolks. Beat egg whites until stiff but not dry; fold half of the whites into the yolk mixture. Fold in remaining egg whites until blended. Spoon this over the applesauce or pipe it from a pastry bag. Set the dish in a pan of very hot water and bake for 45 minutes, until the custard meringue topping is set and lightly browned. Serve warm, with lightly whipped cream if desired.

SHRIMP-SWISS CHEESE FONDUE

2 tbsp. butter
3 tbsp. flour
1 cup Chablis
2 tbsp. lemon juice
1 can frozen cream of shrimp
   soup, thawed
1½ cups grated Swiss cheese

1 (4½ oz.) can cooked shrimp,
   drained and rinsed or 12
   small cooked shrimp
2 tbsp. sherry
Salt (optional)
Cubes of sourdough French
bread

Melt the butter in the fondue pot. Add one tablespoon of the flour and cook the mixture for two minutes, stirring constantly. Do not brown. Add Chablis, lemon juice and soup; heat well. Add the cheese, which has been dredged in remaining two tablespoons of flour, by handfuls, blending each well. Add shrimp and sherry; stir in. Season with salt if desired. Serve with the bread cubes for dunking.

GARDEN SALAD

2 cups diced and drained
   tomatoes
½ cup celery, diced
½ cup green pepper, diced
½ cup cucumber, diced

¼ cup green onion, chopped
2 tbsp. lemon juice
1 tsp. salt
2 tsp. sugar
Pepper to taste

Combine vegetables. Mix lemon juice, salt, sugar and pepper and toss with vegetables. Chill.

Shrimp-Swiss Cheese Fondue
Garden Salad
Green Grapes with
Sour Cream and Brown Sugar
Medium-Dry Sauterne

4 to 6 servings

17

Gorgonzola-Tilsiter Fondue Menu

Gorgonzola-Tilsiter Fondue
Cucumber-Tomato Salad
with Mayonnaise
Cantaloupe with Muscatel

4 to 6 servings

GORGONZOLA-TILSITER FONDUE

⅓ lb. Gorgonzola cheese
⅓ lb. Tilsiter cheese
⅓ lb. Gruyère cheese
3 tbsp. flour
2 cups dry white wine

1 clove garlic, minced
¼ cup kirsch
Salt, pepper and nutmeg to taste
Cubes of sourdough French bread

Grate cheese coarsely and dredge with flour. Heat wine and garlic until almost boiling. Add cheese by handfuls, making sure each addition has melted and blended before adding more. When all the cheese has been added and the mixture is smooth and thick, stir in the kirsch; add nutmeg, salt and pepper. Serve with the bread cubes for dunking.

CANTALOUPE WITH MUSCATEL

2 or 3 cantaloupes, halved and seeded

Muscatel

Prick holes in flesh of the melons with a fork; sprinkle muscatel over so holes absorb it. Refrigerate at least an hour.

POTATO-CHEESE FONDUE

4 medium potatoes, peeled and
    sliced
3 cups water
1 tbsp. butter
1 tbsp. flour
1½ cups milk

½ cup (4 oz.) coarsely grated
    Sbrinz or Spalen cheese
    (Parmesan or Romano can be
    substituted)
2 egg yolks
    Salt, cayenne pepper and
    marjoram

Cook the potatoes in three cups water until mushy. Drain potatoes, reserving water; sieve potatoes. Melt butter in saucepan; add flour and cook without browning for a minute or two. Stir in potatoes with reserved water and milk; blend until smooth and simmer for 10 minutes, stirring occasionally. Add the cheese and beat in the yolks. Continue beating until the mixture is smooth, hot and thick. Add a pinch of salt and cayenne. Crumble a pinch of marjoram over the top.

Note: Good dippers for this unusual fondue include bread; cooked turkey or ham cubes; tiny cooked meatballs; raw cauliflowerets, cherry tomatoes, zucchini or sliced carrots.

Potato-Cheese Fondue
Tossed Salad with
Oil and Vinegar Dressing
Raspberry Sherbet

4 to 6 servings

19

HorseradisH FonduE
Menu

Horseradish Fondue
Vegetable Salad with
Avocado Dressing
Lemon Sherbet

4 to 6 servings

HORSERADISH FONDUE

1 tbsp. butter
½ lb. coarsely grated New York
sharp Cheddar cheese
⅓ cup milk
1 tbsp. Worcestershire sauce
2 tsp. prepared horseradish

Salt and pepper
1 tbsp. flour
2 tbsp. water
2 tbsp. dry sherry
Cubes of sourdough French
bread

Melt butter and cheese together in fondue pot. Add milk, seasonings and flour mixed with water; stir well over low heat until mixture is smooth and thick. Stir in sherry. Serve with the bread cubes for dunking.

Note: This is also good as a cocktail dip with vegetables such as celery, cauliflower, mushrooms, carrots, cherry tomatoes, cucumber, Bermuda onion, artichoke hearts, boiled beets or green pepper; or use with shrimp, cocktail hot dogs or small meatballs.

VEGETABLE SALAD WITH AVOCADO DRESSING

2 or 3 kinds of greens
1 tbsp. minced chives or onions
Radishes
Tomatoes, cut in eighths
2 hard-cooked eggs, chopped
1 carrot, finely minced

Cauliflowerets
Diced cucumber
1 avocado, peeled and pureed
1 cup mayonnaise
Salt and lemon juice to taste

Combine first eight ingredients. Mix avocado, mayonnaise, salt and lemon juice; pour dressing over vegetables.

TOMATO AND BLUE CHEESE FONDUE

1 (10½ oz.) can condensed
    tomato soup
½ cup crumbled blue cheese
1½ cups (6 oz.) chopped sharp
    American cheese

1½ tsp. Worcestershire sauce
¼ cup golden sherry
    Cubes of sourdough French
    bread

Heat the soup and blue cheese. When cheese has melted, add American cheese and Worchestershire sauce. Stir in sherry and blend well. Heat through. Serve with the bread cubes for dunking.

Note: This is good with cooked shrimp as well as bread.

MARINATED MUSHROOM SALAD

Large, firm mushrooms, sliced
French dressing
Chopped chives

Chopped parsley
Lettuce cups

Marinate mushrooms in French dressing, chives and parsley. Serve in lettuce cups.

MERINGUES

2 egg whites
    Pinch salt
¼ tsp. cream of tartar
1 tsp. lemon juice
½ cup sugar

½ tsp. vanilla
1 qt. strawberries, washed,
    sliced and sweetened to taste
1 cup heavy cream, whipped

Preheat oven to 300°. Beat egg whites with salt until frothy; add cream of tartar and lemon juice and beat until stiff. Beat in sugar one tablespoon at a time and continue beating five minutes until very stiff and glossy. Beat in vanilla. Cover a cookie sheet with heavy brown paper or parchment and spoon meringue into little mounds or force through a pastry tube. Shape cups with spoon. Bake for about 30 minutes, until set and lightly browned. Remove from paper while hot and cool on racks. Serve filled with sweetened strawberries and topped with whipped cream.

Tomato and Blue Cheese Fondue
Marinated Mushroom Salad
Meringues with Strawberries
and Whipped Cream

4 to 6 servings

More Cheese Fondues

HOT CHEDDAR FONDUE

1 lb. coarsely chopped sharp
   Cheddar cheese
3 tbsp. flour or cornstarch
1 tsp. dry mustard

¼ tsp. paprika
2 cups dry beer
½ tsp. prepared horseradish
   Cubes of sourdough French
   bread

Dredge cheese in a mixture of the flour, mustard and paprika. Heat the beer in the fondue pot with the horseradish. When almost boiling, stir in the cheese by handfuls, making sure each addition is melted before adding more. Taste for seasoning and add salt or more horseradish if desired. Serve with the bread cubes for dunking.

QUICK FONDUE

1 (11 oz.) can condensed
   Cheddar cheese soup
1 clove garlic, minced

½ cup beer or dry cider
   Chopped chives
   Cubes of sourdough French
   bread

Heat soup, garlic and beer together until very hot. Garnish with chives. Serve with the bread cubes for dunking.

CLASSIC FRENCH FONDUE

2 cups dry white wine
2 cloves garlic, chopped
¾ lb. Emmenthaler cheese,
   coarsely chopped or grated
3 tbsp. cornstarch
2 to 6 tbsp. heavy cream

2 tbsp. butter
3 tbsp. kirsch
   Salt, pepper and nutmeg to
   taste
   Cubes of sourdough French
   bread

Boil wine and garlic briskly in saucepan until wine is reduced to 1½ cups. Strain into fondue pot and discard garlic. Dredge cheese in cornstarch. Reheat wine almost to boiling and add the cheese by handfuls, blending each addition well. When all the cheese has melted and blended, add cream, starting with two tablespoons, until mixture is of the proper consistency. Stir in butter. Stir in kirsch and seasonings, a pinch of each seasoning at first. Serve with the bread cubes for dunking.

TOASTED SESAME SEED CHEESE FONDUE

Toast ½ cup sesame seeds in a large frying pan until they just begin to turn color. Let them cool off in the pan. Grind them quickly in a blender and add to Classic French Fondue (see page 22) or Classic Swiss Fondue (see page 10). Add salt if necessary.

TOASTED ALMOND CHEESE FONDUE

Blanch ¼ cup almonds and toast them in a slow oven. Grind in a blender and add to Classic French Fondue (see page 22) or Classic Swiss Fondue (see page 10). Add salt if necessary.

MEXICAN CHEESE FONDUE

2 cups dry beer	3 tbsp. flour or cornstarch
1 lb. coarsely chopped hot pepper cheese	¼ tsp. salt Cubes of sourdough French bread

Heat the beer in the fondue pot until almost boiling. Dredge cheese in flour; add gradually, stirring after each addition until it is completely melted. When well blended, season with salt. The fondue is quite hot and would serve well as an appetizer. Besides bread cubes, try dunking celery stalks or smoked sausage.

DELICIOUS CLAM FONDUE

1 (8 oz.) can minced clams	1 lb. Emmenthaler cheese, coarsely grated
2 cloves garlic	
1½ cups Chablis	3 tbsp. cornstarch Cubes of sourdough French bread

Drain the clams, reserving the liquor. Put the liquor into the fondue pot with the garlic and wine. Heat almost to boiling; remove garlic. Add Swiss cheese, which has been dredged in cornstarch, by handfuls, blending each addition well. Add clams. Heat thoroughly. Serve with the bread cubes for dunking.

More Cheese Fondues

LOBSTER FONDUE

1 clove garlic, slivered
2 cups Chablis
1 lb. coarsely grated Gruyère cheese
3 tbsp. flour or cornstarch

1 (5½ oz.) can lobster meat or 6 oz. cooked lobster meat, finely chopped
¼ cup Pernod
Salt and cayenne pepper to taste (optional)
Cubes of sourdough French bread

Rub the inside of the fondue pot with garlic pieces; discard garlic. Add the Chablis and heat until almost boiling. Dredge cheese in flour; add by handfuls, blending each addition well. Add lobster meat and Pernod. Taste for seasoning and add the salt and cayenne if desired. Serve with the bread cubes for dunking.

SPINACH FONDUE

1 clove garlic, slivered
2 cups dry white wine
1 lb. coarsely chopped or grated Gruyère or Emmenthaler cheese
3 tbsp. flour or cornstarch
¼ cup kirsch

½ of 10-oz. pkg. frozen chopped spinach (prepared according to pkg. directions)
Pinch rosemary
Salt (optional)
Cubes of sourdough French bread

Rub the inside of the fondue pot with garlic pieces; discard garlic. Add the wine and heat until almost boiling. Dredge cheese in flour; add by handfuls, blending each addition well. When all the cheese is blended, stir in kirsch and well-drained spinach. Crumble the rosemary and stir it in. Taste for seasoning and add salt if desired. Serve with the bread cubes for dunking.

Pictured on the following pages:
Seafood Fondue (page 37)
Oyster Bisque (page 65)
Hawaiian Sauces (pages 56, 57, 67)
Chocolate Ice Cream Fondue (page 91)

24

HERB FONDUE

Classic Swiss Fondue   1 tbsp. fresh chervil
(see page 10)   1 tbsp. fresh tarragon
1 tbsp. fresh parsley   1 tbsp. fresh chives

Prepare Classic Swiss Fondue. Chop herbs finely together; add to fondue.

SWISS-CHEDDAR FONDUE

1 large clove garlic, halved   3 tbsp. flour
1½ cups dry beer or dry   ½ tsp. salt
   white wine   ¼ tsp. pepper
½ lb. sharp Cheddar cheese,   Dash Tabasco sauce
   coarsely grated   Sourdough pumpernickel bread
½ lb. Emmenthaler (Swiss) or   Sourdough French bread
   Gruyère cheese, coarsely
   grated

Rub the inside of the fondue pot with garlic. Heat the beer almost to boiling. Dredge cheese in flour; add by handfuls, blending each addition well. Add seasonings; serve with chunks of sourdough pumpernickel and sourdough French bread.

DANISH CHEESE FONDUE

2 cups dry beer   3 tbsp. flour
1 clove garlic, slivered   Pinch dry mustard
1 lb. Caraway Danbo, Samsoe or   ¼ cup kirsch
   Tybo cheese, grated (natural   Cubes of sourdough French
   caraway cheese, Kuminost, can   bread
   be substituted)

Heat the beer and garlic almost to boiling in the fondue pot. Remove the garlic. Add cheese, which has been dredged in flour, by handfuls, blending each addition well. Add mustard and kirsch. Heat well. Serve with the bread cubes for dunking.

BLUE-CHEDDAR FONDUE

1½ cups beer
¼ tsp. salt
1 tsp. grated onion
¼ cup (2 oz.) crumbled blue cheese

¾ lb. coarsely grated Cheddar cheese
2 tbsp. flour
Cubes of sourdough French bread

Heat beer, salt and onion in the fondue pot. When hot, add blue cheese and stir until it has melted. Dredge cheese in flour; add by handfuls, blending each addition well. Serve with the bread cubes for dunking.

CAERPHILLY FONDUE

1½ cups light dry ale or beer
1 minced shallot or ½ tsp. each minced onion and garlic
2 cups chopped Caerphilly cheese

3 tbsp. flour
Cayenne pepper and salt to taste
Cubes of sourdough French bread

Heat the ale and shallot almost to boiling. Strain into fondue pot, discarding shallot. Dredge cheese in flour; add by handfuls, blending each addition well. Season with cayenne and salt. Serve with the bread cubes for dunking.

Note: This one is for Caerphilly lovers only; if you prefer a more standard fondue, substitute Cheddar.

SMOKE FONDUE WITH SMOKED OYSTERS

1 (8 oz.) container smoke cheese
  spread
½ cup milk

1 (3⅔ oz.) can smoked oysters,
  thoroughly drained
Pinch cayenne pepper

Heat the cheese spread and milk together in fondue pot. When melted, add the oysters. Heat thoroughly. Add cayenne.

Note: This is good as an appetizer or cocktail dip, served with bread cubes; or try butter-baked bread sticks for dipping. For these, place bread sticks on large square of aluminum foil; dribble clarified butter over all. Seal foil into packet and bake at 350° for 20 minutes or until heated through.

ITALIAN FONDUE

1 lb. Italian Fontina or Bel
  Paese cheese, coarsely
  chopped
  Milk
2 tbsp. butter
  Salt and white pepper

3 egg yolks
2 tbsp. flour (optional)
2 tbsp. water (optional)
  French bread triangles, toasted
1 canned white truffle, sliced
  as thin as possible (optional)

Put the cheese in a bowl and cover with milk. Let stand in a cool place (bottom shelf of refrigerator) for 12 hours or overnight. Put the cheese and milk into fondue pot with butter and seasonings. Melt. When thoroughly melted, remove from heat and let cool a few moments. Then quickly beat in the egg yolks with a wire whisk, one at a time, and return to very low heat (use an asbestos pad) for a few moments. If not thick enough, stir in two tablespoons flour blended with two tablespoons water and cook until thickened. Have ready a dish with toasted bread in the bottom for each person. When cheese mixture is hot again, pour a portion into each dish and garnish top with truffle slices.

Note: This is appealing as an appetizer or main course.

27

Fondues without Beer or Wine

CREAMY ITALIAN FONDUE

2 cups whipping cream
4 tbsp. butter
2 cloves garlic, minced
6 flat anchovy fillets, drained, rinsed and finely chopped
1 canned white truffle, minced (optional)
1 tbsp. cornstarch
1 tbsp. water
Vegetables (see below)

Over medium heat reduce the cream to one cup. Put the butter in the fondue pot. When hot, sauté the garlic and anchovies for about two minutes (never letting them brown) until the anchovies disintegrate. Add the cream, truffle and cornstarch blended with water. Bring to a simmer and serve at once with vegetables such as celery, cauliflower, mushrooms, carrots, cherry tomatoes, cucumber, Bermuda onions, artichoke hearts, boiled beets and green pepper.

CIDER FONDUE

1 lb. coarsely chopped sharp Cheddar cheese
3 tbsp. flour or cornstarch
1 tsp. dry mustard
2 cups dry cider
¼ cup applejack or kirsch
Cubes of sourdough French bread

Dredge cheese in flour and mustard. Put cider in the fondue pot; heat until almost boiling. Add cheese by handfuls, making sure each addition has melted and blended before adding more. When all the cheese has been added and the mixture is smooth and thick, stir in applejack. Serve with the bread cubes for dunking.

Note: This is good with fried bread and tart green apple slices as well as sourdough French bread cubes.

DEVILED HAM FONDUE

1 (4½ oz.) can deviled ham
½ cup condensed cream of mushroom soup
½ cup dairy sour cream
¼ tsp. dry mustard
Dash garlic powder
Cubes of sourdough French bread

Combine all ingredients except bread and heat very slowly. Serve with the bread cubes for dunking.

Note: This is a good appetizer-type fondue.

28

SWISS CHEESE AND TOMATO JUICE FONDUE

2 cups tomato juice
1 clove garlic, halved
1 lb. coarsely grated Swiss cheese
1 tbsp. cornstarch or flour
1 tsp. salt
½ tsp. Worcestershire sauce
½ tsp. oregano or basil
¼ tsp. pepper
Dash nutmeg
2 tbsp. cornstarch
2 tbsp. water
Cubes of sourdough French bread

Heat tomato juice and garlic in fondue pot until almost boiling; discard garlic. Cook over low heat or use a double boiler. Add cheese, which has been dredged in cornstarch, by handfuls, making sure each addition has melted and blended before adding more. When all the cheese has been added and the mixture is smooth and thick, add salt, Worcestershire, oregano, pepper, nutmeg and cornstarch blended with two tablespoons water. Cook until the mixture is a smooth blend. Serve with the bread cubes for dunking.

EGG FONDUE

½ cup butter (1 stick)
¼ cup flour
½ tsp. salt
½ tsp. pepper
½ tsp. dry mustard
1 tsp. parsley flakes
Dash Tabasco sauce
2 cups milk
4 egg yolks, slightly beaten
¾ cup grated Parmesan or Romano cheese
Cubes of sourdough French bread

Melt butter in fondue pot and add flour. Cook, stirring constantly, for two minutes. Do not brown. Add salt, pepper, dry mustard, parsley, Tabasco and milk. Cook until thickened and smooth. Pour some of the hot sauce into the egg yolks and blend well. Add the egg mixture to the remaining sauce and cook until thickened. Add cheese and blend well. Serve with the bread cubes for dunking.

Cheese Chart

Cheese	Description	Cheese	Description
BEL PAESE	A popular Italian table cheese. Soft, mild and sweet.	**FONTINA**	Italian sweet, delicate cheese. Made from whole cow's or ewe's milk. Also comes in semi-hard variety, which has a nutty flavor.
BRICK	Native American cheese. Mild and firm when young; acquires an earthy flavor as it ages. Softer than Cheddar, firmer than Limburger; has small holes.	**GERVAIS**	French cream cheese; also known as Petit-suisse.
CAERPHILLY	Welsh semi-hard cheese with a slightly acid, yeasty taste something like that of butter-milk. Best when aged.	**GORGONZOLA**	Italian soft and creamy cheese; white shot with blue. Spicy, piquant flavor.
CHEDDAR	English cheese; white, colored orange. Nutty, tangy, rich and well aged.	**GRADDOST**	Danish semi-firm cheese. Mild and sweet, with a few irregular holes.
DANBO	Danish semi-hard cheese. Nutty in flavor, with small holes.	**GRUYÈRE**	French or Swiss hard cow's milk cheese; has small holes.
EMMENTHALER	Also known as Swiss cheese. Named for the Emmenthal Valley in Switzerland. Flavor is something like that of walnuts or hazelnuts. Holes vary greatly in size.	**HOT PEPPER**	American pasteurized process cheese, seasoned with green chili peppers.
		KUMINOST	Norwegian cheese somewhat like Cheddar, but seasoned with caraway and cumin.

CHEESE CHART

Cheese	Description	Cheese	Description
MONTEREY JACK	American Cheddar-type cheese made from whole or partially skimmed milk. No coloring added.	SAPSAGO	Swiss hard, dried cheese seasoned with powdered clover leaves. Light green in color; sharp, pungent flavor. Also called Schabzieger or Glarnerkäse.
MUENSTER	French semi-hard, fermented cheese with bright red rind.	SBRINZ	Switzerland's oldest cheese. Resembles Gruyère but is harder, with few, if any, very small holes.
PARMESAN	Italian cheese. Hardest of all cheeses when properly cured.		
RICOTTA	Italian rich, creamy, fresh cheese. Usually made from cow's milk.	SPALEN	Swiss hard cheese made with cow's milk. Very similar to Sbrinz but a younger variety. Sharp, nutty flavor.
ROMANO	Italian hard cheese made from cow's, ewe's or goat's milk. Usually grated.	SWISS	See Emmenthaler.
ROQUEFORT	French blue-veined, creamy cheese made wholly from ewe's milk. Well-aged, with a sharp, distinctive flavor.	TILSITER	German medium-firm cheese with small holes. Somewhat like Brick. Light yellow with mild to medium-sharp taste.
SAMSOE	Danish cheese. Rich, golden, somewhat like Cheddar but with the nutty flavor of Emmenthaler.	TYBO	Danish cheese of the Samsoe family. Firm texture with red rind.

Meat and Seafood Fondues

Meat fondue bears slight resemblance to cheese fondue—in fact, they are alike only insofar as they are both cooked and enjoyed at the dinner table by a number of people. If you've never before plunged cubes of uncooked meat or seafood into the bubbling golden depths of a fondue pot, then twirled them into a complementary sauce, and savored the delicious results, we confidently predict that you have a real treat in store.

Vegetable or peanut oil is your best bet for the cooking. (Olive oil tends to impose its own flavor on that of the food; butter will scorch at the high temperature needed to cook the meat.) Arrange an assortment of dipping sauces around the fondue pot.

Each guest spoons sauces onto his own plate, then cooks his cube of meat. (Four to six people is a good number for a fondue party —unless you are using more than one pot—with four cooking at the same time. This prevents overcrowding the pot and lowering the temperature of the oil.) Full instructions for the cooking of beef fondue are given with the main recipe, on page 34.

We start this chapter with the Classic Beef Fondue; it's the basic recipe on which most of the menus are based. And what menus! Most are international in theme, and we think you'll be "sold" on the whole meat fondue idea once you've browsed through these pages and seen how versatile a recipe it is—how many other recipes and themed parties can be built around it. A few examples: the French fondue party includes recipes for Roquefort Turnovers, Chervil, Périgueux and Béarnaise Sauces, and Poached Pears with Crème Anglaise; the Mexican menu features recipes for Seviche, Salsa Verde, Guacamole and Cuernavaca Sauces and Acapulco Soufflé.

Dunk, dip and enjoy! We think you'll agree that meat and seafood fondues form a whole new dimension in eating pleasure—and in party-giving!

Classic
Beef Fondue

2 to 3 lbs. lean tender beef
Parsley or watercress
Peanut oil

Cut the meat into ¾- to 1-inch cubes or in thin strips (allow about a half pound for each serving); arrange on platters on beds of parsley or watercress.

Heat the oil on the kitchen range to 375°; transfer it to a metal fondue pot. Fill the pot no more than half full to avoid bubbling over when the meat is cooked.

Each person spears and cooks his own pieces of meat in the bubbling oil. (Be sure to provide each guest with a long-handled fondue fork for cooking; meat is transferred to dinner fork before it is eaten.) Serve with an assortment of sauces (see following menus for suggestions).

4 to 6 servings.

FONDUE BOURGUIGNONNE
MENU

MUSHROOMS À LA GRECQUE

2 cups water
6 tbsp. olive oil
⅓ cup lemon juice
½ tsp. salt
1 small onion, minced
4 sprigs parsley

1 small celery stick
Pinch thyme
1 tsp. peppercorns
1 lb. fresh button mushrooms
2 tbsp. chopped parsley

Combine water, olive oil, lemon juice, salt, onion, four sprigs parsley, celery, thyme and peppercorns. Simmer for 15 minutes. Add mushrooms and toss. Cover and simmer 10 minutes. Remove to bowl with slotted spoon; reduce remaining liquid to ½ cup and pour over mushrooms. Chill at least eight hours. Sprinkle with chopped parsley before serving.

CHEESE STICKS

1 cup butter (2 sticks) cut in
    ½-inch pieces
1½ cups flour
½ cup ice water

½ cup grated Cheddar cheese
    or Graddost (at room
    temperature)
1 egg beaten with 2 tsp. water
    Poppy seed

Cut butter into flour. Add water to make dough ball. Chill three hours. Preheat oven to 350°. Roll dough to ⅛-inch thickness. Repeat twice more, using ⅓ the cheese each time. Cut into 2½ × ½-inch sticks. Brush with egg; sprinkle with poppy seed. Bake on ungreased sheet for 20 minutes until golden.

CHORON SAUCE

Combine 1 cup Béarnaise Sauce (see page 41) with ¼ cup thick tomato puree or tomato paste.

APPLE HORSERADISH

2 apples, peeled and grated
6 tbsp. prepared horseradish,
    moisture squeezed out

Brown sugar to taste

Mix the apples and horseradish. Add sugar one tablespoon at a time until the desired sweet-sour effect is reached.

Iced Dry Vermouth
Mushrooms à la Grecque
Cheese Sticks
Classic Beef Fondue (see page 34)
Choron, Apple Horseradish,
El Diablo, Mornay Sauces
Garlic Bread
Salad with Lemon Mayonnaise
Coffee Gelatin (see page 13)
Red Burgundy or Red Rhône

4 to 6 servings

35

EL DIABLO SAUCE

1 cup (8 oz.) tomato puree
1 small hot green chili pepper, chopped, seeded and membranes removed
1½ tsp. olive oil
1½ tsp. red wine vinegar
¼ tsp. oregano
¼ tsp. cumin powder
Pinch each ground cloves and garlic salt

Place all ingredients in blender for a few seconds. If you do not have a blender, chop the pepper very finely, then combine with other ingredients and beat by hand or with electric mixer. If too hot (it should be quite hot), cut with a little salt.

MORNAY SAUCE

2 tbsp. butter
2 tbsp. flour
1 cup scalded milk
3 shallots, minced
1 egg yolk
¼ cup grated Parmesan cheese
2 tbsp. dry white wine
Salt (optional)

Make a roux of the butter and flour. Cook five minutes over low heat (use asbestos pad to prevent browning). Add milk quickly, stirring constantly. Add shallots. Cook over low heat for 20 minutes, stirring often. Strain and return to saucepan. Quickly whisk in egg yolk. Over low heat add cheese and wine and cook until smooth. Add salt if necessary. Serve at once.

GARLIC BREAD

Preheat oven to 375°. Split a loaf of French bread lengthwise. Toast cut sides under broiler until golden. Rub each toasted side with ½ clove garlic. Spread softened butter over bread and heat until bubbly.

SALAD WITH LEMON MAYONNAISE

Tomato slices
Minced mushrooms
Mayonnaise
Lemon juice
Lemon slices
Chopped parsley

Combine tomato slices and minced mushrooms; mix with mayonnaise flavored with lemon juice. Top with tissue-thin slices of lemon and chopped parsley.

Seafood Fondue
Menu

EGGS IN ASPIC

4 hard-cooked eggs
1 scant tbsp. gelatin
¼ cup cold water
1 can chicken consommé
1 tbsp. dry Madeira
4 small parsley sprigs
4 slices cooked ham
Bibb lettuce

Shell eggs carefully. Soak gelatin in ¼ cup water to soften. Mix with chicken consommé over low heat until dissolved. Add Madeira. Pour about ¼ inch into bottoms of ramekins. Chill in freezer until set. Place parsley sprigs on top of chilled consommé, then eggs (one in each ramekin), then more heated consommé. Top each with a round of ham and glaze with last of consommé. Chill six hours; unmold onto Bibb lettuce.

SEAFOOD FONDUE

2 to 3 lbs. seafood (shrimp, oysters, chunks of firm-fleshed fish, scallops)
Parsley or watercress
Peanut oil

Allow about a half pound of seafood for each serving; arrange on platters on beds of parsley or watercress.

Heat the oil on the kitchen range to 375°; transfer it to a metal fondue pot. Fill the pot no more than half full to avoid bubbling over when the seafood is cooked.

Each person spears and cooks his own pieces of fish in the bubbling oil. (Be sure to provide each guest with a long-handled fondue fork for cooking; fish is transferred to a dinner fork before it is eaten.) Serve with sauces given in menu.

SAZERAC LOUIS SAUCE

1 cup mayonnaise
¼ cup chili sauce (unsmoked)
1 tbsp. lemon juice
2 drops Angostura bitters
2 drops Peychaud bitters
⅓ cup heavy cream, whipped
Dash Worcestershire sauce

Mix mayonnaise, chili sauce, lemon juice and bitters. Stir in cream and Worcestershire. Chill several hours.

Dry Madeira
Eggs in Aspic
Seafood Fondue
Sazerac Louis, Brown,
Foolproof Hollandaise or Piquant,
Green Goddess
or Rémoulade Sauces
Sesame Vinaigrette Salad
Crusty Rolls
Buttermilk Sherbet
Pouilly-Fuissé

4 to 6 servings

BROWN SAUCE

1½ tbsp. butter	2 cups canned beef consommé
1½ tbsp. flour	1 bouillon cube

Melt butter; add flour and cook, stirring constantly, over low heat until browned. Combine consommé with bouillon cube; stir into roux. Bring sauce to a boil and simmer for 30 minutes, stirring occasionally. Skim off fat as it accumulates (if any does); sieve sauce through strainer lined with a triple layer of cheesecloth.

Note: If you want to save time, prepare a packaged brown sauce instead of using this recipe.

FOOLPROOF HOLLANDAISE SAUCE

3 egg yolks	Lemon juice
1 tbsp. water	Salt
1 cup butter (2 sticks) at room temperature	Cayenne or white pepper

Ahead of time: In the top of a double boiler beat the egg yolks and the water over barely simmering water until light and fluffy. Cut each stick of butter into three pieces. Add four pieces of butter, one at a time, beating hard after each addition, until the eggs incorporate the butter and the sauce is thick. Turn off heat.

At serving time, reheat sauce and add the remaining butter a piece at a time, again beating hard. Season with about one teaspoon lemon juice, a little salt and a few grains pepper.

PIQUANT SAUCE

6 tbsp. dry white wine	1½ tbsp. finely minced sour gherkins
1 generous tsp. minced shallot	
1 cup Brown Sauce (recipe above)	1 tbsp. each chives and parsley Pinch finely chopped tarragon

Cook the wine and shallot until liquid is reduced one third. Add the Brown Sauce; bring to a boil. Turn off for five minutes. Boil again; stir in seasonings and remove from heat.

GREEN GODDESS SAUCE

1 very ripe avocado
1 cup mayonnaise
½ cup sour cream
¼ cup minced parsley
1 tbsp. white vinegar
1 tbsp. tarragon vinegar

1 (2 oz.) can flat anchovies, minced
3 tbsp. minced green onions
1 tbsp. lemon juice
1 small clove garlic, crushed
Salt and pepper to taste

Mix all ingredients and chill 24 hours. Remove garlic before serving.

RÉMOULADE SAUCE

1 cup mayonnaise
1 tbsp. chopped parsley
1 tbsp. drained, chopped capers
1 small clove garlic, minced

1 tbsp. chopped cucumber pickles
Pinch dried tarragon
1 tsp. prepared hot mustard
or ½ tsp. anchovy paste
(optional)

Mix all ingredients well. Chill thoroughly.

SESAME VINAIGRETTE SALAD

6 tbsp. vegetable or olive oil
2 tbsp. lemon juice
1 tbsp. sesame seeds, toasted
Romaine lettuce

1 cucumber, peeled and sliced
Boiled potatoes, chilled and cubed

Beat together oil, lemon juice and sesame seeds. Pour over romaine, cucumber and potatoes. Let stand for about two hours before serving.

BUTTERMILK SHERBET

4 cups buttermilk
1½ cups light corn syrup
½ cup lemon juice

6 tbsp. sugar
2 tbsp. grated lemon rind

Combine all ingredients and pour into two refrigerator trays. Freeze until mushy; pour into a chilled bowl and beat with mixer or rotary beater until smooth. Freeze again, then beat again. Repeat twice more. Serve plain or with fresh strawberries, blueberries or peaches.

FRENCH THEME
BEEf FoNdue
MENU

Medium-Dry Sherry
Roquefort Turnovers
Classic Beef Fondue (see page 34)
Périgueux, Chervil, Lovage Butter,
Béarnaise Sauces
Salad Niçoise
Hot French Bread
Poached Pears
with Crème Anglaise
Emilion or Pomerol Bordeaux

4 to 6 servings

ROQUEFORT TURNOVERS

4 cups flour
1 tsp. salt
¼ tsp. sugar
1 cup butter (2 sticks), cut in
½-inch pieces
6 tbsp. shortening
½ cup ice water
¼ cup ice water (in reserve)

8 oz. Roquefort cheese
½ cup butter (1 stick)
1 egg yolk
1 tbsp. cognac
2 tbsp. minced chives
3 tbsp. cream
Egg
Water

Sift flour with salt and sugar. Cut in butter pieces and shortening until mixture has an oatmeal consistency. Don't overdo. Add ½ cup ice water all at once and blend in quickly. Add remaining water one tablespoon at a time, as much as necessary to bring dough together. On a lightly floured board, work the dough to form a ball. Chill three hours.

Mix Roquefort, ½ cup butter, egg yolk, cognac, chives and cream into a paste.

Preheat oven to 425°. Roll out the dough to ⅛-inch thickness. Cut into 2½-inch squares. Put one teaspoon Roquefort filling in each square. Beat an egg with some water and seal the edges into triangles with this mixture. Brush tops with remaining egg. Poke a hole in the top of each turnover to release steam. Bake on the top shelf of oven for 15 minutes. *Yields 60 turnovers.*

Note: These can be made in advance and refrigerated or frozen until baking time.

PÉRIGUEUX SAUCE

2 cups Brown Sauce (see page 38)
⅓ cup dry Madeira
1 tbsp. chopped canned truffle

1 tbsp. truffle liquid
1 tbsp. butter

Reduce Brown Sauce to one cup. (This can be done slowly by heating over low flame for hours or quickly, by boiling about 30 minutes.) Add Madeira and bring just to boil. Remove from heat immediately.

Add truffle, truffle liquid and butter; serve warm.

CHERVIL SAUCE

1 (6 oz.) pkg. Gervais or Philadelphia cream cheese
1 tsp. lemon juice
  Salt (if Philadelphia cream
  cheese is used)

Dash white pepper
6 tbsp. olive or vegetable oil
Dried or fresh chervil

Blend the cheese with lemon juice, salt and pepper. Beat in the olive oil slowly, as if making mayonnaise. Continue beating until fluffy. Mix in about one tablespoon dried chervil or more chopped fresh chervil, bruising the leaves well before adding. Taste for seasoning and chill well.

Note: Chervil is one of the famous *fines herbes;* it is more delicate than parsley.

LOVAGE BUTTER

½ cup lightly salted butter
  (1 stick) at room temperature

1 tbsp. lime juice
1 tbsp. dried lovage

Cream the butter; add lime juice and lovage. Let mixture stand in a cool place for a few hours (not the refrigerator) to develop the flavors. Refrigerate before serving.

Note: Lovage is a bold herb sometimes substituted for celery in recipes.

BÉARNAISE SAUCE

2 tbsp. white wine
1 scant tbsp. tarragon vinegar
2 tsp. chopped shallots

1 tsp. dried tarragon
  Pinch black pepper
1 cup Foolproof Hollandaise
  Sauce (see page 38)

Combine first five ingredients in a saucepan and boil until almost all liquid disappears. Pour remaining mixture into hollandaise in blender; cover and blend on high speed a few seconds.

French Theme
Beef Fondue
Menu

SALAD NIÇOISE

1 clove garlic, halved
4 heads Bibb lettuce, washed and carefully separated
3 medium tomatoes, peeled and sliced
1 cup cooked and drained green beans
3 medium potatoes, boiled and julienned

4 hard-cooked eggs (whites chopped, yolks sieved)
10 ripe olives, sliced
1 green pepper, diced
1 (7 oz.) can tuna, drained and flaked
6 tbsp. olive oil
2 tbsp. lemon juice
½ tsp. dry mustard
¼ tsp. salt

Rub salad plate with garlic. Arrange lettuce carefully. Arrange tomatoes, green beans, potatoes, egg whites, egg yolks, olives, green pepper and tuna in rows. Beat together olive oil, lemon juice, mustard and salt. Carefully mix salad with dressing at the table.

POACHED PEARS

2½ cups sugar
4 cups water
1 tbsp. vanilla

Large, barely ripe pears, peeled and halved

Dissolve sugar in water and bring to a boil with the vanilla. Add pears and reduce heat. Poach pears in syrup until tender and translucent. Cool and drain pears. Chill well.

CRÈME ANGLAISE

4 egg yolks
½ cup sugar

1½ cups scalded milk
1 tbsp. vanilla

Beat yolks with sugar in top of double boiler. When yolks are beaten and thick, pour in hot milk in a slow, thin stream. Put custard over simmering water and stir until it thickens enough to coat a spoon. Remove from heat and beat for one minute. Strain. Stir in vanilla. Serve warm over cold pears.

PROSCIUTTO WITH FIGS

Use fresh figs if possible—otherwise canned, not dried. Allow two or three per person. Wrap with prosciutto ham and garnish with mint sprigs. Serve on watercress.

Note: If you prefer to make Lamb Fondue, follow the recipe on page 34, substituting lean lamb for the beef.

SKORTHALIA

6 cloves garlic
1 tsp. salt
6 slices stale white bread or 4
  medium potatoes, peeled,
  boiled and cooled

2 cups olive oil
½ cup wine vinegar

Peel the garlic and pound in mortar with salt until it is a smooth pulp. Add the bread or potatoes and olive oil alternately. When blended, stir in the vinegar.

Note: If bread is used, wet the slices first in a little water and squeeze dry. This will work if the bread is really stale; otherwise it will be difficult because of preservatives. If bread doesn't seem stale enough, potatoes would be a better choice for this sauce.

ATHENS MINT

1 tbsp. mint leaves
1 tbsp. tomato paste

1 cup Foolproof Hollandaise
  Sauce (see page 38)

Chop mint leaves and place in boiling water for about five minutes. Drain well. Add to the tomato paste and combine with hollandaise. Taste for seasoning.

ROSEMARY BUTTER

2 tsp. rosemary
½ cup unsalted butter (1 stick)
  at room temperature

2 tbsp. lemon juice

Crush and chop the rosemary very fine. Cream the butter and blend in the lemon juice. Add crushed rosemary. Let the butter stand in a cool place (not the refrigerator) for a few hours to develop the flavors. Sieve the butter and chill before serving.

Ouzo
Prosciutto with Figs
Classic Beef Fondue (see page 34)
Skorthalia, Athens Mint,
Rosemary Butter, Mykonos Sauces
Greek Potato Salad
Ambrosia
Red Bordeaux or Red Rhône

4 to 6 servings

43

MYKONOS SAUCE

1 tbsp. butter
1 small onion, minced
1 tbsp. flour

1 cup strong chicken stock (dissolve 2 chicken bouillon cubes in 1 cup water)
Grated rind of ½ lemon
Juice of ½ lemon

Heat butter. Sauté onion; sprinkle in flour when onion is transparent. Stir and cook for about two minutes over low heat; do not brown. Stir in chicken stock and lemon rind. Bring to a boil and simmer 20 minutes. Strain, pressing down hard on solids to extract juices. Add lemon juice. Serve hot.

GREEK POTATO SALAD

1 lb. cooked, diced potatoes (cooled)
1 small onion, grated
1 tsp. oregano (¼ tsp. if dried)
12 Greek or black olives, chopped

2 hard-cooked eggs, chopped
¼ cup olive oil
2 tbsp. lemon juice
Salt and pepper
Diced tomato

Combine all ingredients except diced tomato; garnish with tomato.

AMBROSIA

2 large oranges, peeled and sectioned (white removed)
3 ripe bananas, sliced thinly
2 tbsp. Grand Marnier

¼ cup confectioners' sugar
1 cup shredded coconut
Mint

Sprinkle fruit with liqueur and sugar. Arrange in layers with coconut between each layer in bowl. Garnish with mint.

JAPANESE TIDBITS

1 cup soy sauce
½ cup dry sherry
  Pinch powdered ginger
1 tsp. grated onion
¼ lb. mushroom caps
¼ lb. filet of beef, cut in
  ½-inch cubes

¼ lb. boneless chicken breast,
  cut in ½-inch pieces
¼ lb. shelled shrimp, cut in
  ½-inch pieces
  Tiny broiling onions

Boil together soy sauce, sherry, ginger and grated onion for two minutes. Marinate mushroom caps, beef, chicken, shrimp and onions in mixture in refrigerator for six hours or overnight. Thread solid ingredients on small bamboo skewers; broil, basting with remaining marinade.

Dry Sherry
Japanese Tidbits
Classic Beef Fondue (see page 34)
Dragon, Black Bean with Garlic,
Mandarin's Dream, Teriyaki Sauces
Rice Molds
Japanese Salad
Hot Curried Fruit
Fortune Cookies
Cabernet Rosé, Rheinpfalz or
Rhône

4 to 6 servings

DRAGON SAUCE

¼ cup dry mustard   ½ to 1 cup boiling water

Place mustard in top of double boiler. Add enough boiling water to make the consistency you want. Let stand over barely simmering water 15 to 20 minutes to develop flavor.

BLACK BEAN WITH GARLIC SAUCE

1 clove garlic, minced
3 green onions, finely chopped
2 tbsp. vegetable oil
1 tbsp. black bean spice
  (obtainable at Chinese stores)
  or cooked black beans

1 tsp. cornstarch
½ cup water
1 tsp. soy sauce

Sauté garlic and onions in oil until tender. Add bean spice (if using beans, crush them with a fork). Stir in cornstarch blended with water and soy sauce. Cook three minutes.

45

Oriental Theme
Beef Fondue
Menu

MANDARIN'S DREAM

1 small green pepper, seeded and minced
1 small yellow onion, minced
2 tbsp. vegetable oil
¾ cup chicken stock (dissolve 1 chicken bouillon cube in ¾ cup water)
½ cup canned pineapple juice
½ tsp. soy sauce
½ tsp. molasses
½ tsp. Chinese brown sauce (obtainable at Chinese stores)
1 tsp. cornstarch
1 tbsp. water

Sauté green pepper and onion in oil. Add remaining ingredients except cornstarch and water. Simmer for 10 minutes. Stir in cornstarch blended with water. Cook until thickened. Serve hot or warm.

TERIYAKI SAUCE

1 cup dry sherry or dry Madeira
½ cup soy sauce
¼ tsp. grated ginger or pinch powdered ginger
1 tbsp. sugar

Bring all ingredients to a boil in saucepan. Let simmer until reduced to one cup.

RICE MOLDS

½ cup rice, steamed until done
⅔ cup chopped parsley

Mix the rice with the parsley and pack the mixture into buttered ramekins. Keep hot in a pan of shallow water in hot oven. Unmold at serving time (will not unmold perfectly).

JAPANESE SALAD

¼ cup rice wine vinegar (mirin)
  or wine vinegar
1 scant tbsp. sugar
1 head iceberg lettuce, torn in
  bite-size pieces

8 thin slices cucumber
4 cooked, peeled and deveined
  shrimp, cut in half

Mix vinegar and sugar; toss with other ingredients.

HOT CURRIED FRUIT

1 cup sugar
2 cups water
2 tsp. vanilla
1 cup fresh pear slices (barely
  ripe)
1 cup fresh pineapple chunks

1 cup fresh peach slices
½ cup firmly packed brown sugar
⅓ cup melted butter
1 tbsp. curry powder
  Vanilla or coconut ice cream

Dissolve sugar in water; add vanilla. Bring to a boil and boil for five minutes. Add fruits and poach until tender. Drain and arrange fruit in baking dish. Sprinkle with brown sugar, butter and curry powder. Bake uncovered in 300° oven for one hour. Serve with vanilla or coconut ice cream on the side.

Note: If you use canned fruit in this recipe, omit poaching in sugar syrup.

Mexican Theme
Beef Fondue
Menu

Sangría
Seviche
Classic Beef Fondue (see page 34)
Mexican Guacamole,
Cuernavaca Mayonnaise,
Salsa Verde,
Guacamole del Diablo Sauces
Orange-Onion Salad
Hot Buttered French Rolls
Acapulco Soufflé
Châteauneuf-du-Pape

4 to 6 servings

SANGRÍA

½ cup lemon juice
¼ cup orange juice
½ cup sugar

4/5 qt. red table wine
Lemon slices or thin orange
wedges

Combine lemon and orange juice and sugar. Strain. Add wine. Serve in tall glasses half filled with crushed ice. Garnish with lemon slices or thin orange wedges.

SEVICHE

1 lb. firm-fleshed fish (such as
striped bass or red snapper)
1½ cups lime juice
½ cup grapefuit juice
½ cup chopped onions

1 chopped green chili pepper
2 chopped, seeded tomatoes
2 tsp. salt
¼ tsp. Tabasco sauce
Pinch oregano

Marinate fish in remaining ingredients for at least 12 hours in glass bowl in refrigerator. Drain before serving. The acidity "cooks" the fish, but if you are at all squeamish, or think your guests may be, poach the fish until barely done before marinating.

MEXICAN GUACAMOLE

1 medium avocado, very ripe
1 tsp. lime juice
1 medium tomato, peeled,
seeded and chopped
1 small onion, grated

1 tsp. chili powder (or to
taste)
1 tbsp. olive oil
½ tsp. coriander powder
Salt and pepper to taste

Mash the avocado with the lime juice until very smooth. Add remaining ingredients and mix.

CUERNAVACA MAYONNAISE

1 cup mayonnaise
¼ cup chili sauce (unsmoked)
2 tbsp. tomato paste
1 tbsp. each tarragon, vinegar
and chives

1 tsp. each onion juice and
Worcestershire sauce
Salt and pepper to taste

Blend all ingredients well.

SALSA VERDE

1 bunch watercress (leaves only)
1 cup parsley sprigs
2 small cloves garlic
  Salt

6 tbsp. olive oil
2 tbsp. lime juice
  Mayonnaise

Chop the watercress, parsley and garlic together with a generous pinch of salt until almost liquid. Add the oil in a thin stream, beating well, as if making mayonnaise. Add lime juice and taste for seasonings. Stir in just enough mayonnaise to bind.

GUACAMOLE DEL DIABLO SAUCE

2 ripe avocados
1 small hot green chili pepper
1½ tbsp. minced onion
1 clove garlic, minced

2 tbsp. lime juice
1 tsp. salt
1 ripe tomato, peeled, seeded
  and minced

Place all ingredients but tomato in blender and blend until combined; or beat in mixing bowl. Stir in tomato.

ORANGE-ONION SALAD

Large Bermuda or Spanish
onion
2 cups ice water
1 tsp. salt

2 large oranges, sectioned
  or sliced (white removed)
6 tbsp. olive oil
2 tbsp. tarragon vinegar
½ tsp. salt

Slice onion thin and soak slices in ice water and one teaspoon salt. Drain after 10 minutes and combine with orange sections. Beat olive oil, vinegar and ½ teaspoon salt together well; pour over onion and oranges.

ACAPULCO SOUFFLÉ

1 cup water	2 tbsp. flour
¾ cup brown sugar	5 eggs
¾ cup granulated sugar	½ lb. Monterey Jack or Brick
¼ cup rum	cheese, grated finely
2 tbsp. butter	Cinnamon

Butter a 2-quart soufflé dish and coat the inside with sugar. Boil water, brown and granulated sugars and rum for five minutes. Cool. Melt butter; add flour and cook for two minutes, stirring constantly. Do not brown. Separate eggs; beat yolks until thick and add to cooled sugar-water mixture. Stir in flour-butter mixture and cheese; heat until mixture begins to boil and thickens. Stir constantly. Cool. (The soufflé can be made in advance to this point. An hour before serving dessert, continue with the remaining steps.) Preheat oven to 350°. Beat egg whites until stiff but not dry. Combine half of the egg white mixture with the yolk mixture. Fold in the remainder of the egg whites. Pour into soufflé dish. Sprinkle with cinnamon. Bake for 45 minutes. Serve at once.

VEGETABLE TRAY WITH DILL DIP

Make a dill dip with sour cream, chopped dill and salt to taste. Serve with radishes, cauliflower, cherry tomatoes (halved and seeded for easier eating), carrots, celery and scallions. Arrange attractively on a tray. Also on tray: herring fillets, thin slices of pumpernickel, sweet butter and small glasses of aquavit.

NORWEGIAN TOMATO BUTTER

½ cup butter (1 stick) at room temperature
2 tbsp. tomato paste
½ tsp. salt
¼ to ½ tsp. sugar (or to taste)

Cream the butter in a small bowl until very fluffy. Continue creaming and add tomato paste gradually. When well blended, add salt and ¼ tsp. sugar. Taste for seasonings and add more sugar if desired. Chill well before serving.

Note: Here is an attractive way to serve the tomato butter: Cut a tomato into thick slices. Remove pulp and leave each circle of tomato intact. Place tomato circles on sheet of waxed paper and pack butter mixture inside. Chill. Remove from paper with spatula.

NORWEGIAN HORSERADISH BUTTER

½ cup butter (1 stick) at room temperature
2 tbsp. prepared horseradish
½ tsp. salt
Lemon juice

In a small bowl, cream the butter until very fluffy. Add horseradish, salt and few drops lemon juice. Blend well. Chill well before serving.

SWEDISH MUSTARD

4 tbsp. dark prepared mustard
1 tsp. mild dry mustard
2½ tbsp. sugar
2 tbsp. white wine vinegar
⅓ cup vegetable oil
3 tbsp. chopped fresh dill or
½ to 1 tsp. dried dill

Combine the mustards. Add sugar and vinegar. Mix well. Beat in oil very slowly. When thoroughly blended, add the dill.

Aquavit
Vegetable Tray with Dill Dip
Classic Beef Fondue (see page 34)
Norwegian Tomato Butter,
Norwegian Horseradish Butter,
Swedish Mustard,
Danish Blue Cheese Sauces
Mushroom-Cucumber Salad
Caramelized Potatoes
Strawberry Pudding
Aquavit and Beer or Red Bordeaux

4 to 6 servings

51

Scandinavian Theme
Beef Fondue
Menu

DANISH BLUE CHEESE SAUCE

½ cup crumbled Danish blue cheese
½ cup sour cream

Large pinch dried thyme or 1 tsp. fresh chopped thyme
Few drops lemon juice

Blend cheese and sour cream well. Mix in thyme, bruising the leaves well before adding. Add lemon juice to taste.

Note: Domestic blue cheese or Roquefort can be used instead of the Danish blue.

MUSHROOM-CUCUMBER SALAD

½ lb. mushroom caps
1 large cucumber
6 tbsp. salad oil

2 tbsp. mild white vinegar
½ tsp. salt
1 tbsp. minced chives

Mince mushrooms. Peel and seed cucumber; slice thinly. Beat oil, vinegar and salt together. Mix with mushrooms and cucumber; chill until serving time. Garnish with chives.

CARAMELIZED POTATOES

24 very small new potatoes
4 tbsp. butter

1 to 2 tbsp. brown sugar

Boil potatoes in jackets (or use large potatoes, quartered). When done, drain and peel. Keep warm.

In a saucepan, heat butter and brown sugar together until hot and bubbly. Add potatoes; shake pan to coat them with the hot caramel.

52

STRAWBERRY PUDDING

1½ qts. strawberries
⅓ cup sugar
1½ tbsp. gelatin
½ cup cold water
2 cups sweetened whipped cream

1 (10 oz.) jar raspberry jelly
2 tbsp. kirsch
4 thinly sliced bananas
Blanched slivered almonds

Puree 1 qt. strawberries. Add sugar and let stand three hours. Soften gelatin in scant ½ cup cold water. Dissolve over hot water. Stir into puree and chill. When it begins to thicken, fold in cream. Oil an 8-cup ring mold. Pour in berry cream and chill six hours. Melt raspberry jelly with kirsch. Glaze bananas and remaining berries. Chill fruits. Unmold cream and fill center with fruit. Sprinkle with almonds.

Russian Theme
Beef Fondue
Menu

Champagne
Zakuski
Classic Beef Fondue (see page 34)
Apple-Vodka Mayonnaise,
Samovar Horseradish, Caviar Butter,
Stroganoff Sauces
Beet-Raisin Salad
Black Bread
Moscow Cheese and Grape Tart
or Cherries Jubilee
Châteauneuf-du-Pape

4 to 6 servings

ZAKUSKI

Chopped chicken livers
Matjes herring
Potato salad with mushrooms
Smoked salmon

Black bread, thinly sliced
Cream cheese
Radishes, celery and carrots
Sour cream-onion dip

Arrange all ingredients on a large platter.

APPLE-VODKA MAYONNAISE

3 medium green apples, peeled,
    cored and chopped
½ cup water

2 tbsp. brown sugar
1 jigger vodka
Mayonnaise

Stew apples in ½ cup water until mushy. Strain into serving bowl. Mix in sugar and vodka. Mix with equal amount mayonnaise.

SAMOVAR HORSERADISH

½ cup prepared red horseradish
1 tsp. dry mustard

1 tsp. sugar
Salt to taste

Combine all ingredients. (Use sparingly; it's hot!)

CAVIAR BUTTER

½ cup sweet butter (1 stick)
    at room temperature

3 tbsp. caviar
2 tbsp. lemon juice

Cream butter. Mix in caviar and lemon juice. Chill well before serving.

STROGANOFF SAUCE

1 tbsp. butter
1 small onion, minced
1 small clove garlic, minced
2 tbsp. tomato puree

Salt and pepper
1 cup sour cream
1 tbsp. sherry

Melt butter in saucepan, add onion and garlic and sauté until onion is transparent. Add tomato puree, salt, pepper, sour cream and sherry. Simmer for 15 minutes.

54

BEET-RAISIN SALAD

1 cup pickled beets, julienned	6 tbsp. salad oil
¾ cup raisins, plumped in hot	2 tbsp. lemon juice
water	½ tsp. salt
Lettuce	½ tsp. dry mustard
Watercress	

Drain beets and raisins. Arrange on a bed of lettuce and watercress. Mix oil, lemon juice, salt and mustard together well; pour over beets and raisins.

MOSCOW CHEESE AND GRAPE TART

Pastry for two-crust 9-inch pie	1 egg yolk
1 pint creamed small-curd	2 tbsp. sugar
cottage cheese	⅛ tsp. salt
2 tbsp. butter	½ cup sour cream
2 eggs, separated	½ cup grape conserve

Preheat oven to 350°. Line pan with half of pastry. Cream together all ingredients except conserve. Pour into shell. Spread conserve over filling. Top with lattice crust. Bake for 30 to 40 minutes. Serve cool or cold.

CHERRIES JUBILEE

3 (4 oz.) bottles pitted white	1 cup sugar
cherries or 2 cups pitted	¼ cup kirsch
Bing cherries	6 tbsp. cognac
1 tsp. arrowroot	Granulated sugar
1 tsp. lemon juice	Vanilla ice cream

Drain the juice from the cherries and put it in the blazer pan of a chafing dish (use a medium-size frying pan if you don't have a chafing dish). Mix the arrowroot and lemon juice together and add this and one cup sugar; reduce the mixture to a thick syrup over high heat, stirring constantly. Let simmer (best over boiling water) for 15 minutes. Add cherries during final five minutes. Add prewarmed kirsch and cognac. Sprinkle the surface with granulated sugar (don't stir in). Stand back and ignite. Serve flaming over ice cream.

Hawaiian Theme
Beef Fondue
Menu

Dry Madeira
Coconut Chips
Shrimp Salad
Classic Beef Fondue (see page 34)
Hawaiian Apricot Supreme,
Curried Cream (see page 67)
Hawaiian Sweet-Sour,
Waikiki Sauces
Hawaiian Salad with
Thousand Island Dressing
Refreshing Rum Sop
Cabernet Rosé

4 to 6 servings

SHRIMP SALAD

1 lb. green shrimp, shelled and deveined
1 bottle white wine or 3 (12 oz.) cans beer
½ clove garlic
Pinch oregano
1-inch piece bay leaf
3 hard-cooked eggs (whites chopped, yolks sieved)
4 scallions, chopped
Mayonnaise
Worcestershire sauce
Salt to taste

Simmer shrimp in wine, garlic and herbs until done. Combine egg whites and scallions; mix with the drained shrimp together with enough mayonnaise to coat. Add egg yolks, mayonnaise, Worcestershire sauce and salt to salad; mix.

HAWAIIAN APRICOT SUPREME

1 (10 oz.) jar apricot jam
⅓ cup white vinegar
¼ tsp. salt
2 tbsp. honey
1 tbsp. paprika

Heat jam in top of double boiler, over boiling water, until very hot. Add vinegar, salt, honey and paprika. Mix well and let stand over simmering water for about 20 minutes to develop flavor. Serve warm.

Note: This sauce is extremely good with pork too.

HAWAIIAN SWEET-SOUR SAUCE

1½ tsp. cornstarch
3 tbsp. water
6 tbsp. white vinegar
½ cup sugar
3 tbsp. Worcestershire sauce
3 tbsp. catsup
1 tsp. salt

Make a paste from the cornstarch and water. Combine with all other ingredients in a saucepan. Heat, stirring constantly, until slightly thickened. Serve warm.

WAIKIKI SAUCE

¾ cup fresh pineapple, finely
chopped or slivered (or un-
sugared canned pineapple)

2 tbsp. butter
¼ cup crushed macadamia nuts

Sauté pineapple in butter until golden and soft. Add nuts and mix well. Serve warm.

HAWAIIAN SALAD

1 head romaine, rinsed and
torn in 1-inch pieces
1 can hearts of palm, drained
and rinsed

1 green pepper, minced
Thousand Island Dressing
(below)

Combine romaine, hearts of palm and green pepper; serve with Thousand Island Dressing.

THOUSAND ISLAND DRESSING

1 cup mayonnaise
¼ cup chili sauce
2 tbsp. minced stuffed olives
1 tbsp. pickle relish

1 tbsp. chopped green pepper
1 tbsp. minced chives or onion
1 tbsp. chopped parsley
1 hard-cooked egg, chopped

Combine all ingredients; chill.

REFRESHING RUM SOP

1 cup water
1 cup rum
2 cups sugar
½ cup each finely diced
pineapple and banana

Raspberry sherbet
Whipped cream, sweetened
and flavored with vanilla
½ cup blanched, slivered and
toasted almonds

Make a syrup by boiling water, rum and sugar for five minutes. Remove from heat and pour over fruit. Let mixture marinate 12 to 24 hours in refrigerator. At serving time, drain fruit and spoon it over servings of sherbet. Top with cream and almonds.

British Theme
Beef Fondue
Menu

Potted Cheese with
Assorted Tea Biscuits
Classic Beef Fondue (see page 34)
Pub, Chestnut Crème,
Keswick Herb Cream,
Cumberland Sauces
Welsh Leek Salad
English Muffins
Special Strawberries
English Ale

4 to 6 servings

POTTED CHEESE

1 lb. very sharp Cheddar cheese   ½ cup finely chopped unsalted
Heavy cream   pistachios
¼ cup dry Madeira

Grate cheese; beat in cream and wine and stir in nuts. Pack into buttered bowl and chill. Remove from refrigerator one hour before serving. Unmold like gelatin. Garnish with pistachios. Serve at room temperature.

PUB SAUCE

⅓ cup dry white wine   1 (6 oz.) can tomato paste
8 peppercorns, crushed   ½ cup raisins
2 shallots, chopped   1 tsp. Worcestershire sauce
1 cup Brown Sauce (see page 38)   ½ tsp. chopped parsley

Cook the wine, peppercorns and shallots in saucepan until only one tablespoon wine remains. Add Brown Sauce, tomato paste, raisins and Worcestershire. Simmer about 30 minutes, adding a bit more wine if the mixture seems too thick. Strain, pressing down on solids to extract all juices. Correct seasonings. Garnish with parsley.

CHESTNUT CRÈME

1 strip bacon   2 tbsp. butter at
½ cup boiling water   room temperature
¼ cup canned chestnuts, sieved   1 tbsp. vermouth
2 oz. double cream cheese or   ½ tsp. salt
    Philadelphia cream cheese

Blanch the bacon in boiling water for five minutes. Remove from water and drain. Cook until crisp and crumble into pieces. Combine chestnuts, cream cheese and butter; blend well (add some milk or cream if the consistency is too thick). Add vermouth, salt and bacon. Chill well before serving.

58

KESWICK HERB CREAM

2 tbsp. butter
2 tbsp. flour
1 cup heavy cream
½ cup sour cream
¼ cup ground English walnuts
½ tsp. dried dill

Pinch each dried basil, tarragon and chives
1 tsp. coriander powder
Pinch garlic powder or ½ clove garlic, minced
Few grains cayenne pepper
Salt to taste

Blend butter and flour and cook 10 to 15 minutes, stirring constantly until browned. Stir in creams, which have been heated together. Bring to a simmer; simmer for three minutes. Add walnuts, herbs and seasonings; simmer two minutes more.

CUMBERLAND SAUCE

6 shallots
Rinds of 1 orange and 1 lemon
1 (10 oz.) jar tart red currant jelly

⅓ cup tawny port or claret
2 tsp. wine vinegar
Juice of ½ orange and ½ lemon

Parboil the shallots for a few minutes; peel and mince. Cut the thinnest possible rind from the fruit, carefully omitting any of the white, and cut rind into thin strips. In top of double boiler melt jelly and add port. Add vinegar and rinds, shallots and juices. Cook over boiling water 10 minutes until rinds are just tender. Serve chilled.

WELSH LEEK SALAD

8 leeks, split lengthwise
2 hard-cooked eggs (whites chopped, yolks sieved)
Generous pinch dried tarragon
Pinch dried sweet basil
1 tbsp. chopped parsley

1 tbsp. drained capers
3 tbsp. white wine vinegar
½ cup olive oil
Salt and pepper
1 tbsp. chopped chives

Parboil the white parts of the leeks for 10 minutes. Chill thoroughly. On serving plates, arrange pieces of leeks. Sprinkle with egg whites, herbs and capers. Combine wine vinegar, olive oil, salt and pepper; pour over leeks. Garnish with sieved yolks and chives.

British Theme
Beef Fondue
Menu

ENGLISH MUFFINS

1 envelope yeast
¼ cup warm water
1 cup scalded milk
3 tbsp. butter
2 tbsp. sugar

1 tsp. salt
4 cups sifted flour
1 egg, slightly beaten
Cornmeal

Dissolve yeast in water. Mix milk with butter, sugar and salt; heat until butter melts. Cool to 85°. Add to the milk two cups flour, yeast and egg. Beat thoroughly. Add remaining flour to make medium-soft dough. Knead until smooth. Place in buttered bowl; butter top, cover and let rise until doubled, about an hour. Punch down; let rest for 15 minutes. Roll out on board sprinkled with cornmeal to ¼-inch thickness. Cut into 3-inch rounds. Cover and let rise until doubled again, about 45 minutes. Heat an ungreased griddle or electric fry pan to very hot. Reduce heat to medium and place rounds on griddle. Brown them slowly, about 7 minutes on each side. Cool; split, toast and butter.

SPECIAL STRAWBERRIES

1 qt. hulled fresh strawberries,
  sliced thin
Brown sugar

1 cup whipping cream
Granulated sugar
2 to 3 tbsp. port

Sprinkle berries with brown sugar and refrigerate for several hours. Whip cream until stiff. Add granulated sugar to taste. Fold in port. Serve strawberries with port-cream.

PROSCIUTTO AND CANTALOUPE

Cut a chilled cantaloupe into 16 even pieces after seeding. Remove rind and discard. Wrap each melon piece in a small piece of prosciutto ham. Serve chilled, with lemon wedges.

AIOLI SAUCE

2 cloves garlic, minced
Salt
1 egg yolk (at room temperature)
⅔ cup olive oil
Juice of ½ lemon (1 tbsp.)

Place garlic in a mortar or small deep-sided bowl. With a pestle or wooden spoon, begin mashing it, adding salt a pinch at a time until garlic is reduced to a paste. Drop the egg yolk into garlic and mix well. When thoroughly blended and thick, begin adding the oil, drop by drop, whisking fast with a wire whisk. When half the oil has been added in this manner, you can increase the flow to a thin stream—but be careful that all oil is blending in. When as thick as mayonnaise, add lemon juice. Chill slightly.

ITALIAN DIP

1 minced carrot
3 small cloves garlic, minced
½ cup minced onion
¼ cup olive oil
1 large can tomato puree or sauce (4 cups)
1 to 2 tbsp. tomato paste
Oregano or sweet basil
¼ cup freshly grated Parmesan cheese
¼ to ½ cup white wine or dry vermouth

Sauté the carrot, garlic and onion in olive oil until they are soft and lightly browned. Stir in tomato puree, tomato paste, oregano and about ¼ cup Parmesan cheese. Bring this to a boil slowly and simmer for 10 minutes. Stir in wine during the last five minutes.

Medium-Dry Sherry
Prosciutto and Cantaloupe
Classic Beef Fondue (see page 34)
Aioli, Italian Dip, Parmesan Butter, Anchovy Sauces
Hot Buttered Bread Sticks
Lemon Florentine Salad
Venetian Lemon-Lime Ice
Beaujolais

4 to 6 servings

61

PARMESAN BUTTER

½ cup sweet butter (1 stick)   ½ cup grated Parmesan cheese
at room temperature

Cream butter and cheese together. Chill slightly before using.

Note: Sapsago cheese can be used instead of the Parmesan.

ANCHOVY SAUCE

4 tbsp. butter   1 tbsp. capers, minced
¼ cup oil   8 cloves garlic, minced
2 tsp. lime juice   4 oz. anchovy fillets, drained
                                    and rinsed

Heat butter and oil together. Add remaining ingredients and heat, stirring constantly until fillets disintegrate.

LEMON FLORENTINE SALAD

½ lb. mushroom caps   1 tbsp. grated Parmesan cheese
1 lb. young spinach leaves,   1 clove garlic, slivered
washed and stemmed   2 hard-cooked eggs
6 tbsp. vegetable or olive oil   Finely grated rind of ½ lemon
2 tbsp. lemon juice   (white removed)
½ tsp. salt

Slice mushroom caps and combine with spinach. Chill. Beat oil, lemon juice, salt, cheese and garlic. Chop egg whites. Sieve yolks. Remove garlic pieces from dressing after about three hours. Pour dressing over salad; sprinkle with egg white, egg yolk and lemon rind. Toss at the table.

VENETIAN LEMON-LIME ICE

4 cups water   Pinch salt
2 cups sugar   ½ cup lemon juice
1 tbsp. grated lemon rind   ¼ cup lime juice, strained
(white removed)

Make a syrup of first four ingredients. Let boil five minutes. Stir in juices and pour into a freezer tray. Freeze until mushy. Pour into a chilled bowl and beat with a whisk or fork until frothy. Return to tray and freeze until firm.

GERMAN HORS D'OEUVRES

Arrange an assortment of the following on a tray: pickled onions or an onion sliced and marinated in vinegar and salt; thin-sliced roast beef marinated in vinegar and salt; tiny sausages, parboiled and broiled; assorted vegetables with a horseradish-mayonnaise dip.

BAVARIAN HORSERADISH ICE

3 tbsp. prepared horseradish, moisture squeezed out	3 tbsp. freshly squeezed strained orange juice
½ tsp. sugar	1 cup heavy cream, whipped stiff

Combine all ingredients but cream. Fold in cream. Freeze four hours.

TOMATO MAYONNAISE

1 cup mayonnaise	Dash Tabasco sauce
2 tbsp. heavy cream, slightly beaten	1 medium tomato, peeled, seeded and minced
2 tbsp. tomato paste	

Combine ingredients and chill well.

JUNIPER SAUCE

3 hard-cooked egg yolks	10 juniper berries, finely crushed
1 tbsp. prepared sharp mustard	
½ cup vegetable or olive oil	Salt and pepper to taste
1 tbsp. vinegar	Small beets

Rub the yolks through a fine sieve into a small, deep-sided bowl. Blend in mustard. Stir in oil, drop by drop, alternately with the vinegar, beating well after each addition to keep sauce smooth. (This could be done in a blender.) Stir in crushed berries. Season lightly with salt and pepper. Chill about five hours to develop flavor. Taste again and add more salt and pepper if needed. Cook 1 small beet per person in salted water until done. Cut a small slice from the stem end of each beet so it will stand upright; hollow out beets and serve juniper sauce in them.

Iced Vermouth
German Hors d'Oeuvres
Classic Beef Fondue (see page 34)
Bavarian Horseradish Ice,
Tomato Mayonnaise,
Juniper, Wilhelm Sauces
Parsleyed Potatoes (see page 10)
Pumpernickel Rolls
German Chocolate Ice Box Torte
Rhine Wine

4 to 6 servings

63

German Theme Beef Fondue Menu

WILHELM SAUCE

½ cup soy sauce
½ cup sherry or whiskey

2 tbsp. brown sugar
Pinch ginger

Combine all ingredients. Serve with beef which has been topped with dusting of freshly ground pepper after cooking.

GERMAN CHOCOLATE ICE BOX TORTE

1 pkg. German chocolate cake mix
1 pkg. German chocolate icing mix with almonds

1 cup heavy cream, whipped stiff, or 1 carton frozen whipped topping
⅛ tsp. almond extract
½ cup blanched almonds, toasted, then ground in blender

Prepare cake according to package directions. When cool, split layers in half, making four layers. Make the icing. Sweeten whipped cream if necessary and fold in almond extract and ground almonds. Fill layers with the cream mixture and frost top with the icing. Refrigerate until cold (about four hours).

Pictured on the following pages:
Melba Fondue (page 92)
Lemon Florentine Salad (page 62)

64

OYSTER BISQUE

4 tbsp. butter	Pinch nutmeg
1 pint oysters with liquor	Salt and pepper
1 cup milk	Chopped parsley
1 cup light cream	4 tsp. dry sherry or Chablis

Melt butter and sauté drained oysters until edges curl. Add milk, cream, oyster liquor, nutmeg, salt and pepper. Bring just to a boil and ladle into bowls. Sprinkle with parsley and stir in one teaspoon sherry to each serving.

Dry Sherry or Dry Madeira
Oyster Bisque
Classic Beef Fondue (see page 34)
Cointreaumato, Blender Hollandaise,
Summer Mayonnaise,
Pepper Relish Sauces
Buttermilk Biscuits
Garden Salad (see page 17)
Glazed Plum Turnovers
Red Bordeaux

4 to 6 servings

COINTREAUMATO SAUCE

1½ cups red Burgundy	½ cup (4 oz.) tomato paste
2 medium onions, chopped	Tabasco sauce
1 stalk celery, chopped	Salt and pepper
1 cup beef broth	2 tbsp. Cointreau

Combine all ingredients but salt, pepper and Cointreau. Simmer for several hours until reduced by half or boil down to half in about 15 minutes. Strain, pressing down hard on solids to extract juices. Add salt, pepper and Cointreau. Heat for about five minutes.

BLENDER HOLLANDAISE

½ cup butter (1 stick)	¼ tsp. salt
3 egg yolks	Few grains cayenne or pinch
2 tbsp. lemon juice	white pepper

Heat butter until bubbly over low heat. Meanwhile put yolks into blender. Turn on and off quickly. When butter is hot, turn blender on high, remove cover and add hot butter in thin stream. Add lemon juice, salt and pepper. Don't overblend.

Note: For successful results, do not alter the size of this receipe.

SUMMER MAYONNAISE

1 cup mayonnaise	1 tsp. chopped fresh tarragon
1 tbsp. chopped fresh parsley	½ tsp. chopped fresh chervil
2 tsp. chopped fresh chives	½ tsp. chopped fresh dill

Combine all ingredients. Let stand in refrigerator for a few hours (no more than four) before serving.

65

PEPPER RELISH SAUCE

1 cup mayonnaise
⅓ cup sweet pepper relish

2 tbsp. heavy cream, slightly
beaten
1 tbsp. or more lemon juice

Mix all ingredients thoroughly. Chill well.

BUTTERMILK BISCUITS

2 cups sifted flour
3 tsp. baking powder
½ tsp. salt

¼ tsp. soda
5 tbsp. shortening
1 cup buttermilk

Preheat oven to 450°. Sift flour, baking powder, salt and soda; cut shortening into flour mixture to the consistency of coarse cornmeal. Pour in buttermilk and mix with a fork. Form into ball. Knead on floured board for 30 seconds. Roll to ½-inch thickness. Cut into rounds with 1½-inch cutter. Bake for 12 to 15 minutes or until golden.

GLAZED PLUM TURNOVERS

2 lbs. plums, peeled, pitted and
chopped or 1 lb. 13 oz. can
purple plums, drained, pitted
and chopped
½ cup sweetened orange juice
3 tbsp. granulated sugar
1 tbsp. cornstarch

Pinch each cinnamon, nutmeg
and allspice
Pastry for two-crust 9-inch pie
Vegetable oil
1 cup sifted confectioners' sugar
1 tbsp. rum
1 tbsp. light cream

Combine plums with orange juice, granulated sugar, cornstarch and spices. Set aside for 30 minutes while making pastry. After rolling out, cut pastry into 5-inch circles (use a saucer as a guide). Drain plums; place one rounded tablespoon of filling on each circle and seal by dampening edges with water and crimping edges with tines of fork. Fry in deep vegetable oil at 375° for five minutes. Make glaze with confectioners' sugar, rum and cream. Spread on warm turnovers. *Yields 11 turnovers.*

Note: The turnovers can be made in advance and either refrigerated or frozen until ready to deep fry and glaze.

EASY APPLE MAYONNAISE

½ cup apple butter
½ cup mayonnaise
2 tbsp. red wine vinegar

¼ cup lemon juice
Grated rind of ½ lemon
(white removed)

Combine all ingredients.

TARRAGON MUSTARD SAUCE

1 cup mayonnaise
2 tbsp. sour cream
1½ tsp. dry mustard

2 tsp. tarragon vinegar
Salt to taste
⅛ to ½ tsp. dried tarragon

Mix all ingredients well, bruising tarragon leaves well before adding. Chill for a few hours (no more than four) to develop flavors.

MADEIRA MUSHROOM SAUCE

1 lb. mushroom caps
4 tbsp. butter
1 shallot
½ tsp. parsley

⅓ cup dry Madeira
1 cup Brown Sauce (see page 38)
½ tsp. salt
Pinch pepper

Clean and dry mushroom caps and cut into thick slices. In a saucepan melt the butter and sauté mushrooms until golden. Chop shallot and parsley together. Add when the mushrooms are golden and sauté a few moments longer. Add Madeira and Brown Sauce and simmer five to six minutes. Add salt and pepper.

CURRIED CREAM

½ cup mayonnaise
½ cup sour cream

1 to 2 tsp. curry powder
1 tsp. lemon juice

Combine all ingredients. Taste for seasoning. Add more curry powder or lemon juice if desired.

67

MUSTARD SAUCE

2 tsp. prepared mustard
½ cup heavy cream, whipped stiff

Salt, pepper and lemon juice to taste

Combine all ingredients.

ROBUST MUSTARD SAUCE

⅓ cup sour cream
⅓ cup mayonnaise
1 tbsp. dry mustard

1 tbsp. finely minced green onion
1½ tsp. tarragon vinegar
Salt to taste

Combine all ingredients. Serve icy cold.

CITRUS GARLIC SAUCE

5 cloves garlic, minced
5 whole cloves garlic
5 tbsp. olive or vegetable oil
1 cup orange juice

½ cup lemon or lime juice
½ tsp. crushed rosemary
Salt and pepper to taste

Cook the garlic in the oil in a small saucepan. Discard the whole garlic cloves when the minced garlic becomes light brown. Add juices and seasonings and cook over medium heat, stirring constantly, until mixture boils. Boil down to half the amount.

Note: This is a thin sauce.

TIJUANA PEANUTS

½ lb. shelled raw peanuts
Chili powder
Coriander

Salt
Cayenne pepper

If peanuts still have their skins, blanch them for three minutes in boiling water, then plunge into icy water and rub skins off. Spread peanuts on a cookie sheet; place in a 350° oven for about 10 minutes to dry.

Put nuts, a handful at a time, into a blender and grind finely. Spread nuts on a cookie sheet and sprinkle with seasonings to taste. Toast for about 20 to 30 minutes in moderate oven until golden. Shake off excess seasonings.

DRESDEN MAYONNAISE

1 cup mayonnaise
¾ cup slightly sweetened
   whipped cream

Few drops lemon juice
Catsup
1 large or 2 medium oranges

Combine the mayonnaise with the cream by folding lightly. Add a few drops lemon juice and a tablespoon or two of catsup; fold in. Taste. Add more catsup if desired, but not too much. Halve and hollow out orange(s); cut a thin slice at bottom of each half so it will stand upright. Mound the mayonnaise into the orange shells; place in freezer for about an hour before serving.

GARLIC BUTTER

1 to 3 cloves garlic, minced
1 tsp. to 1 tbsp. salt

½ cup sweet butter (1 stick)
   at room temperature

In a small bowl or mortar, mash the garlic together with the salt with a pestle or wooden spoon. Add the butter; cream well. Chill before serving.

SPICED MUSTARD SAUCE

1 cup sour cream
2 tbsp. Dijon-style mustard
1 tbsp. soy sauce
1 tbsp. Worcestershire sauce

1 tsp. grated onion
1 clove garlic, crushed
Salt and pepper to taste

Combine all ingredients and chill for a few hours.

SWEET AND SOUR SAUCE

4 tbsp. butter
¼ cup flour
½ tsp. dry mustard
1¼ cups water
3 tbsp. white wine vinegar

1 tbsp. soy sauce
⅔ cup currant, plum or apple
   jelly
½ cup firmly packed brown sugar

Melt butter; add flour with dry mustard. Cook the mixture for two minutes, stirring constantly. Do not brown. Remove from heat. Add water, vinegar, soy sauce, jelly and sugar. Cook, stirring constantly, until mixture comes to a boil and thickens.

POLISH RAISIN SAUCE

1 tbsp. bacon fat or butter
1 tbsp. flour
1 cup beef stock, canned beef bouillon or bouillon cube dissolved in 1 cup hot water
¼ cup gingersnap crumbs
¼ cup raisins, chopped
1 small onion, stuck with 2 cloves
1 strip lemon rind (white removed)
1 bay leaf
Red wine
Lemon juice
Cinnamon
Salt
Sugar
1 tbsp. Madeira

Melt bacon fat; add flour and cook, stirring constantly, until dark coffee color. Do not scorch. Add stock and bring to a simmer. Add crumbs, raisins, onion, lemon rind and bay leaf. Simmer slowly for 30 minutes. Season to taste, starting with about one tablespoon red wine, ½ teaspoon lemon juice and pinch each of seasonings. Remove onion, lemon rind and bay leaf with a slotted spoon. When seasoning is correct and just before serving, add Madeira.

ORIENTAL MARINADE

1 tbsp. dry mustard
1 tbsp. brown sugar
1 tsp. powdered ginger
1 medium onion, minced
1 cup soy sauce

Combine all ingredients in a saucepan. Heat to boiling and simmer 10 minutes. Let cool somewhat and pour over meat. Marinate 12 hours or overnight in refrigerator.

JAPANESE MARINADE

½ cup soy sauce
¾ cup sake or white wine
1 tbsp. brown sugar
Rind from 1 lemon, cut in 1x¼-inch strips (white removed)
1 small onion, grated
½ tsp. powdered ginger
1 clove garlic, slivered

Combine all ingredients in saucepan. Bring to a boil and simmer 10 minutes. Let cool somewhat and pour over meat. Marinate 12 hours or overnight in refrigerator.

MANDARIN MARINADE

1 tbsp. dry mustard
1 tbsp. brown sugar
2 tsp. powdered ginger
4 scallions, minced
2 cloves garlic, minced
Thumbnail-sized piece of bay leaf
½ cup soy sauce
¾ cup dry sherry

Combine all ingredients and pour over meat. Marinate several hours.

MARINADE FOR PORK

1 cup beer
½ cup salad oil
2 tsp. dry mustard
1 clove garlic, crushed
2 tbsp. lemon juice
1 tsp. sugar
3 cloves

Combine all ingredients and pour over meat. Marinate several hours.

MARINADE FOR LAMB

¾ cup dry red wine
¼ cup olive oil
2 crushed juniper berries
Sprig each parsley and thyme
Thumbnail-sized piece of bay leaf
1 clove garlic, crushed
2 slices onion
1 tsp. salt
⅛ tsp. pepper

Combine all ingredients and pour over meat. Marinate several hours in refrigerator.

SEAFOOD MARINADE

2 tbsp. lemon juice
6 tbsp. salad oil
1 tsp. salt
⅛ tsp. pepper

Beat all ingredients together well. Marinate fish, turning often, for 1½ hours at room temperature.

Special Fondues

Your crowd loves to try anything new—including new recipes. And there's nothing they like better than your fondue parties. But you've run out of ideas. Your faithful pot is fresh out of tricks—or is it?

Here are a few special fondues we'll bet you haven't tried—and your friends haven't tasted. Come up with one of these the next time you plan to get together and watch what happens!

Let's say you've planned an afternoon slaloming down the nearby slopes, or maybe you're involved in a community effort to dig driveways out after a devastating snowstorm. When the mission's accomplished, build up the fire in the fireplace and help the group get thawed out with Raclette. It's quick and easy to fix—and warming. Or choose a dreary day when no special activity is planned, light the candles and introduce guests to Fondue Rapperswil. It'll be a quick trip to Switzerland—minus the air fare!

The Steak-Cheese Specials and the Teriyaki Meatball Fondue would be sure-fire winners to brighten up the otherwise standard fare at a cocktail party; of course, they stand on their own in dinner menus, too!

A side dish of Potato Fondue for any dinner suggests new heights for the ofttimes scorned boiled potato. And when you next think of turkey, don't think of the large Thanksgiving bird, but rather of Batter-Fried Turkey Fondue—a glorious treatment for a year-round favorite and a change of pace for holiday or any-day meals.

Give you some new ideas? Even jaded appetites, we'll venture, will perk up for these. So, don't waste a minute—try them!

Après-Ski
Menu

Raclette
Boiled or Fried Potatoes
Pickled Onion Rings
Valais Wine

RACLETTE

In Switzerland, this is served after skiing. In small inns in Europe, it is served in the afternoon.

In the book *Heidi,* Heidi and her grandfather ate Raclette in front of the fireplace. You too can make it in the fireplace or on the stove or in front of a portable electric heater.

You will need about ½ lb. Gruyère (natural and well-aged) per person or use Muenster, Tilsiter or Monterey Jack. The dish is served with boiled or fried potatoes and pickled onion rings.

A large hunk of cheese is speared on a sturdy fork and held in front of the fire until it begins to melt. The melted part is scraped off onto the hot plate of potatoes and onions. It must be eaten immediately. Valais wine is an excellent accompaniment.

CRABMEAT QUICHE

Pastry for 10-inch quiche pan
2 tbsp. minced green onion
3 tbsp. butter
1 cup cooked crabmeat, drained and diced
¼ tsp. salt
Dash cayenne pepper
2 tbsp. dry vermouth
3 eggs
1 cup evaporated milk or whipping cream
1 tbsp. tomato catsup
Salt and pepper
¼ cup grated Emmenthaler cheese

Prick bottom of pastry with a fork to keep it from rising. Partially bake in a 400° oven for 8 to 9 minutes or until pastry begins to color and shrink from sides. Remove from oven. Turn oven to 375°. Sauté onions in butter until tender but not brown. Add crabmeat, salt, cayenne pepper and vermouth. Bring to a boil and remove from heat.

Beat the eggs, milk and tomato catsup together. Stir in crabmeat mixture. Season to taste with salt and pepper. Pour mixture into partially baked shell. Sprinkle with cheese. Bake for 25 to 30 minutes until quiche is browned.

FONDUE RAPPERSWIL

This fondue is named after a town in Switzerland where it is served.

Fill fondue pot with strong, well-flavored bouillon. Slice beef in paper-thin strips instead of cubes (freeze first for easier cutting).

The meat strips are cooked until done in the boiling bouillon. When all the meat is finished the stock is greatly enriched. Stir in two egg yolks and serve the resulting "egg drop soup" to guests.

CUCUMBER AND DILL SAUCE

1 cup peeled, seeded and diced cucumber
1 cup sour cream
2 tbsp. vinegar
2 tsp. finely chopped fresh dill or ¼ tsp. dried dill
1 tsp. dried onion flakes
¼ tsp. salt
Dash cayenne pepper

Combine all ingredients. Chill.

Riesling
Crabmeat Quiche
Fondue Rapperswil
Cucumber and Dill, Red Velvet,
Noble Mayonnaise,
Polynesian Sauces
Artichoke Salad
Popovers
Flan
Red Bordeaux or Burgundy

4 to 6 servings

FONDUE RAPPERSWIL
MENU

RED VELVET SAUCE

2 tbsp. butter
6 large tomatoes, diced and
   mashed
1 tsp. brown sugar

¾ tsp. salt
¼ tsp. paprika
   Dash cayenne pepper

Melt butter. Add remaining ingredients and cook, stirring constantly, over low heat until the consistency of thick paste. Strain the mixture. Serve warm or cold.

NOBLE MAYONNAISE

1 cup mayonnaise
½ cup red currant jelly
3 tbsp. prepared horseradish
2 tbsp. dry sherry or Madeira

¼ tsp. salt
⅛ tsp. black pepper
½ cup heavy cream, whipped

Combine all ingredients except cream. Mix well. Fold in cream. Chill.

POLYNESIAN SAUCE

1 cup soy sauce
½ cup lemon juice
½ cup dry sherry
¼ cup chopped green onions

1 tsp. grated fresh ginger
½ tsp. sugar
¼ tsp. white pepper

Combine all ingredients. Let stand an hour to blend flavors.

ARTICHOKE SALAD

1 (15 oz.) can (2 cups) artichoke
   hearts, drained and cut in
   half lengthwise

12 cherry tomatoes, cut in half
   Vinaigrette Dressing
   (see page 15)
   Lettuce

Marinate artichoke hearts and tomatoes in Vinaigrette Dressing for two or three hours. Just before serving, drain and arrange on lettuce or in lettuce cups.

POPOVERS

1 cup milk
1 cup flour
1 tbsp. melted butter

¼ tsp. salt
2 eggs

Preheat oven to 475°. Beat milk, flour, butter and salt together just until smooth. Add one egg at a time. Do not overbeat. Fill greased popover tins ¾ full. Bake for 15 minutes. Reduce heat to 350°; do not open oven door. Bake 20 minutes longer. Pierce the popovers with a sharp knife to let the steam escape after baking (this will prevent soggy centers).

FLAN

½ cup sugar
2 tbsp. water
½ cup sugar
3 eggs

3 egg yolks
2½ cups hot milk
1 tsp. vanilla

Preheat oven to 350°. In a 1-quart metal or fireproof mold, boil ½ cup sugar with water until sugar caramelizes. Dip the mold into cold water to cool slightly. Tilt and twist the mold to coat with the syrup. When syrup is set, turn upside down. Gradually beat the second ½ cup sugar into eggs and egg yolks until well mixed. Add hot milk slowly; continue to beat. Stir in vanilla. Strain the mixture through a sieve into caramel-lined mold.

Set in a larger pan; add boiling water to pan to come halfway up its sides. Place in oven and reduce heat to 325°. Keep the water at a simmer during baking. If the water boils, the custard will be grainy. Bake for 40 to 60 minutes or until a knife inserted in the center comes out clean. If you wish to serve custard warm, set in pan of cold water for 10 minutes; chill in refrigerator if you wish to serve it cold. To unmold, run a knife around edge of mold; invert on serving plate.

Steak-Cheese Menu

Dry Madeira
Shrimp Diablo
Steak-Cheese Specials
Smitane, Tarragon Butter,
Chutney, Western Sauces
Baked Potatoes with
Lemon Butter and Caviar
Romaine Salad with Mushrooms
Chocolate Mousse
Cabernet Rosé or
Chateau Prieuré Lichine

4 to 6 servings

SHRIMP DIABLO

1 cup vegetable oil	1 tbsp. paprika
½ cup dry vermouth	1 tsp. salt
½ cup wine vinegar	¼ tsp. cayenne pepper
2 tbsp. prepared mustard	1 clove garlic, minced
2 tbsp. tomato catsup or chili sauce	1 lb. cleaned, cooked shrimp
	Lettuce

Combine all ingredients except shrimp and lettuce. Beat well. Pour dressing over shrimp. Marinate four to six hours in refrigerator. Just before serving, drain shrimp and arrange on lettuce.

STEAK-CHEESE SPECIALS

1 tbsp. tomato paste	Dash pepper
1 tsp. prepared horseradish	½ lb. ground steak
1 tsp. prepared mustard	¼ cup fine soft bread crumbs
1 tsp. minced onion	½ lb. cheese, cut in small cubes (Swiss, blue, Cheddar)
2 tsp. brown sugar	Vegetable oil
1 tsp. vinegar	
½ tsp. salt	

Combine all but last four ingredients; let mixture stand for 30 minutes to develop flavor. Combine the sauce with meat and bread crumbs. Shape the mixture around cheese cubes. Guests spear these and cook in boiling oil for about two minutes.

SMITANE SAUCE

2 small onions, finely minced	1 cup scalded sour cream
1½ tbsp. butter	Salt and pepper
½ cup dry vermouth	1 tsp. lemon juice

Sauté onions in butter until soft but not brown. Add vermouth. Cook, stirring occasionally, until liquid is reduced to almost nothing. Add sour cream and stir until blended. Simmer over very low heat for 5 minutes. Strain the sauce through a fine sieve or cheesecloth. Season to taste with salt and pepper. Just before serving, add lemon juice.

TARRAGON BUTTER

2 tsp. tarragon
½ cup butter (1 stick) at room temperature

1 tbsp. lemon juice

Crush and chop the tarragon very fine. Cream butter and blend in lemon juice. Add tarragon. Let the butter stand in a cool place (not the refrigerator) for a few hours to develop the flavors. Chill before serving.

CHUTNEY SAUCE

¾ cup currant jelly
½ cup Indian chutney

1 tbsp. brandy
Salt

Heat all ingredients except salt in top of double boiler or over very low heat. Season to taste with salt. Serve warm.

WESTERN SAUCE

2 cups chili sauce
2 tbsp. wine vinegar
2 tbsp. soy sauce
1 tbsp. minced onion

1 tbsp. brown sugar
1 tsp. dry mustard
Dash Tabasco sauce

In a saucepan, combine all ingredients. Bring to a boil, stirring constantly. Simmer for 10 minutes. Serve hot or cold.

BAKED POTATOES WITH LEMON BUTTER AND CAVIAR

4 to 6 baking potatoes
Vegetable oil
½ cup butter (1 stick) at room temperature
Rind from 1 lemon, grated (white removed)

1½ tbsp. lemon juice
1 tbsp. grated onion
1 (4 oz.) jar red caviar
Chopped chives

Preheat oven to 375°. Scrub the potatoes and rub with oil. Prick the potatoes with a fork to prevent them from exploding in the oven. Bake for about one hour. Blend butter, grated lemon rind, lemon juice and onion. Serve potatoes with lemon butter, caviar and chives.

STEAK-CHEESE
MENU

ROMAINE SALAD WITH MUSHROOMS

1 head romaine
½ lb. raw mushrooms, washed
  and sliced
8 green onions, finely chopped
6 tbsp. vegetable oil

2 tbsp. vinegar
¼ cup chopped watercress
  or parsley
1 tsp. salt
Pepper to taste

Tear romaine into bite-size pieces. Add mushrooms and onions.
Blend oil, vinegar, watercress, salt and pepper. Just before serving,
toss salad with dressing.

CHOCOLATE MOUSSE

4 eggs, separated
¾ cup superfine sugar
3 tbsp. brandy
1 tsp. vanilla
6 oz. or squares semisweet
  chocolate

4 tbsp. strong coffee
4 tbsp. butter at room
  temperature
1 tbsp. superfine sugar
Whipped heavy cream
(optional)

In the top of a double boiler, beat the egg yolks, ¾ cup sugar
and brandy until the mixture is thick and pale yellow. Place over
barely simmering water; continue beating for four to five minutes. Then beat over cold water until the mixture cools and is
the consistency of mayonnaise. Beat in vanilla.

Melt chocolate and coffee over very low heat or in top of
double boiler. Remove from heat; gradually stir in butter. Beat
the chocolate mixture into egg yolks. Beat the egg whites until
foamy; sprinkle with one tablespoon sugar and continue beating
until stiff peaks form. Stir ¼ of the egg whites into the chocolate
mixture. Fold in remaining whites until no streaks remain. Spoon
the mousse into a 2-quart serving dish or individual dessert cups.
Chill four hours or overnight. Serve with whipped cream if
desired.

Pictured on the following pages:
British Theme Beef Fondue (pages 34, 58)
Strawberry Pudding (page 53)

ORIENTAL CHICKEN WINGS

12 chicken wings	1 tbsp. oil
1 tsp. salt	¾ cup orange marmalade
3 tbsp. butter	¼ tsp. ground ginger

Cut the wings in half, discarding tips. Season with salt. Heat butter and oil in skillet; add wings. Sauté about 20 minutes or until evenly browned. Add marmalade and ginger. Cook, turning often, for 20 more minutes. Drain on paper towels. Serve hot.

TERIYAKI MEATBALL FONDUE

1 tbsp. soy sauce	1 clove garlic, crushed
1 tbsp. water	½ lb. ground steak
2 tsp. sugar	½ cup fine soft bread crumbs
½ tsp. minced onion	Vegetable oil

Combine soy sauce, water, sugar, onion and garlic; let stand 30 minutes to develop flavor. Mix ground steak and bread crumbs together; combine thoroughly with soy sauce mixture. Form into ¾-inch balls and spear on bamboo skewers. Cook less than two minutes in boiling oil.

TANGY TOMATO SAUCE

2 (6 oz.) cans tomato paste	1 tsp. salt
1 cup beef broth	¼ tsp. black pepper
1 tbsp. Worcestershire sauce	Dash cayenne pepper
2 tsp. caper liquid	2 tbsp. capers

In a saucepan, combine all ingredients except capers. Bring to a boil, stirring constantly. Simmer for 10 minutes. Add capers. Serve hot or cold.

BLACK CURRANT SAUCE

⅔ cup black currant jam	½ cup chopped black walnuts
3 tbsp. lime juice	

Heat jam and lime juice slowly until jam melts. Add walnuts. Serve warm.

Dry Sherry
Oriental Chicken Wings
Teriyaki Meatball Fondue
Tangy Tomato, Black Currant, Chive,
Pacific Sauces
Snow Peas and Water Chestnuts
Mandarin Orange Salad with
Honey Dressing
Pineapple Sherbet with
Almond Cookies
Cabernet Rosé or Rhône

4 to 6 servings

81

Oriental Fondue
Menu

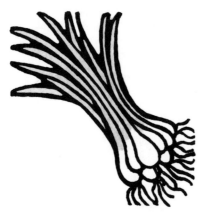

CHIVE SAUCE

2 egg yolks
2 tbsp. lemon juice
1 tsp. salt
Dash cayenne pepper

1½ cups vegetable oil
½ cup chopped chives
½ cup chopped parsley
1 tbsp. minced onion

Beat egg yolks until frothy. Add lemon juice, salt and cayenne pepper. Beat in ½ cup oil, a teaspoon at a time. Add remaining oil more quickly, beating until thick. Stir in chives, parsley and onion. Serve chilled.

PACIFIC SAUCE

½ cup soy sauce
½ cup lemon juice
½ cup dry sherry

½ cup chili sauce
½ cup creamy peanut butter
½ cup chopped green onions

Combine all ingredients and let stand for a few hours to develop the flavors.

SNOW PEAS AND WATER CHESTNUTS

3 (10 oz.) packages frozen snow peas, thawed
1½ cups green onions, sliced diagonally into 1-inch pieces

¼ cup vegetable oil
1 (5 oz.) can water chestnuts, drained and sliced
2 tsp. salt

Dry snow peas on paper towels. Sauté onions in hot oil for one minute. Add snow peas, water chestnuts and salt. Cook, stirring constantly, for two or three minutes until very hot and lightly browned.

Note: Snow peas are flat, pale-green peas eaten pods and all; they are sold fresh by weight in Oriental specialty shops. If you're using fresh rather than frozen snow peas in this recipe, buy 1½ pounds. Wash and dry them, removing tips and side strings.

82

MANDARIN ORANGE SALAD WITH HONEY DRESSING

2 (8 oz.) cans mandarin orange segments, chilled and drained	Lettuce Honey Dressing (below)

Arrange orange segments on lettuce; serve with Honey Dressing.

HONEY DRESSING

½ cup honey
½ cup lime juice

Dash ground ginger

Combine all ingredients. Chill.

ALMOND COOKIES

¼ cup butter	½ tsp. almond extract
¼ cup shortening	1 egg yolk
1 cup flour	1 tbsp. water
6 tbsp. sugar	24 blanched almond halves
½ tsp. salt	

Cut butter and shortening into flour until crumbs are very fine. Add sugar, salt and almond extract. Blend well. Shape into long rolls, one inch in diameter; wrap in waxed paper. Chill one hour.

Preheat oven to 400°. Cut each roll into ¼-inch slices. Place one inch apart on greased cookie sheet. Brush with mixture of beaten egg yolk and water. Press ½ almond into top of each cookie. Bake for 8 to 10 minutes until light golden brown. *Yields 2 dozen cookies.*

Note: The dough can be made in advance and refrigerated or frozen until needed.

Potato Fondue
Menu

STUFFED MUSHROOMS

1 lb. large mushrooms
¼ cup vegetable or olive oil
¼ cup minced onion
1 clove garlic, minced
½ cup finely chopped turkey
½ cup fine dry bread crumbs
2 tbsp. grated Parmesan cheese
1 egg
1 tbsp. chopped parsley
½ tsp. oregano
Salt and pepper to taste
Butter

Preheat oven to 325°. Wash mushrooms; remove stems and reserve. Sauté whole mushroom caps in oil until coated with oil and lightly colored. Drain. Chop stems to make ½ cup; sauté with onion and garlic, adding more oil if necessary. Simmer for 10 minutes. Stir in turkey, bread crumbs, Parmesan cheese, egg, parsley, oregano and salt and pepper. Spoon the mixture into mushroom caps. Dot with butter. Bake for 30 minutes.

BRAISED LAMB

4- to 5-lb. lamb shoulder or
  leg of lamb, boned
2 tbsp. prepared mustard
  (optional)
¼ tsp. ground thyme (optional)
⅛ tsp. garlic powder (optional)
3 tbsp. vegetable or olive oil
1 cup chopped onion
1 cup chopped celery
1 cup chopped carrot
2 cups beef broth
1 cup dry vermouth
½ cup fresh parsley
½ cup celery leaves
2 tsp. salt
½ tsp. black pepper
¼ tsp. garlic powder
¼ tsp. ground thyme
¼ tsp. Tabasco sauce
2 tbsp. cornstarch
2 tbsp. water
Salt and pepper

Rub lamb shoulder cavity with mustard, ¼ tsp. thyme and ⅛ tsp. garlic powder. Roll and tie. (If you buy a boned and rolled shoulder, omit seasonings.) Preheat oven to 350°. Brown lamb evenly in oil in a Dutch oven. Remove. Sauté onion, celery and carrot in drippings until tender. Return meat to Dutch oven. Add beef broth and vermouth. Liquid should half cover meat. Add next seven ingredients. Bring to a boil.

Bake, covered, for 2½ to 3 hours or until tender. The braising liquid should simmer at all times. Add more broth if necessary. When done, remove lamb from pan. Strain broth; discard vegetables and remove excess fat from pan. Thicken broth with cornstarch and water. Cook, stirring constantly, until thickened. Season to taste with salt and pepper. Serve sauce with the lamb.

POTATO FONDUE

20 small new potatoes
¾ cup safflower oil
1¼ cups cider vinegar

1 large onion, minced
2 tsp. salt

Peel the potatoes and cook until done in boiling salted water. Combine oil, vinegar, onion and salt in a metal fondue pot. Cook over high heat until the onion is transparent. Place sauce over warmer and keep hot over low flame. Dip hot cooked potatoes into sauce.

ESCAROLE SALAD WITH BEETS

1 cup diced cooked beets
1 cup diced onion
1 head escarole or romaine, torn
    into bite-size pieces
1 cup yogurt

2 tbsp. mayonnaise
1 tsp. sugar
Dash lemon juice
Salt and pepper

Combine beets, onion and escarole. Blend yogurt, mayonnaise, sugar and lemon juice. Season to taste with salt and pepper. Just before serving, toss salad with yogurt dressing.

ITALIAN BREAD

½ cup butter (1 stick) at room
    temperature
½ cup chopped parsley

¼ cup sesame seeds
1 loaf Italian bread, cut in
    half lengthwise

Preheat oven to 375°. Combine butter, parsley and sesame seeds. Spread on bread halves. Re-form loaf and bake for 15 minutes.

Note: If desired, grated Cheddar, Gruyère, Monterey Jack or Parmesan cheese may be added to the sesame butter.

HONEYDEW MELON WITH PORT

1 or 2 honeydew melons, chilled   Port

Serve ¼ to ⅓ melon per person, depending on size of melon. Just before serving, add one or two tablespoons port to each portion of melon.

Turkey Fondue Menu

Dry Madeira
Cream of Asparagus Soup
Batter-Fried Turkey Fondue
Sweet and Sour (see page 69),
Elegant Cranberry,
Horseradish Cream,
Tomato Sauces
Wild Rice
Orange and Onion Salad
Pumpkin Parfait Pie
Red Bordeaux or
Pinot Chardonnay

4 to 6 servings

CREAM OF ASPARAGUS SOUP

1 (1 lb.) can (2 cups) asparagus tips
Milk
2 tbsp. butter
2 tbsp. flour
¼ tsp. salt
¼ tsp. celery seed
1 hard-cooked egg, chopped

Drain asparagus, reserving liquid. Add enough milk to liquid to total three cups. Melt butter; add flour, salt and celery seed. Cook, stirring constantly, for two minutes. Do not brown. Gradually add milk mixture and cook until thickened. Puree asparagus in blender (or use a strainer). Add sauce and blend until smooth. Return to saucepan; reheat slowly for about five minutes. Serve garnished with chopped hard-cooked egg.

BATTER-FRIED TURKEY FONDUE

½ cup milk
1 egg
1 tbsp. vegetable oil
¾ cup flour
1½ tsp. baking powder
½ tsp. salt
3½ cups cooked turkey or pork cubes
Vegetable oil

Combine milk, egg and one tablespoon oil; beat well. Add flour, baking powder and salt, mixing until smooth. Each guest spears a turkey cube on his fondue fork, then dips it into batter, making sure all sides are coated. The coated meat is then fried in a fondue pot in hot oil (400°) until well browned.

ELEGANT CRANBERRY SAUCE

1 cup granulated sugar
1 cup water
2 cups cranberries, washed and with stems removed
4 tbsp. orange marmalade
1 tbsp. lemon juice
1 cup chopped blanched almonds

In a saucepan, combine sugar and water; stir to dissolve sugar. Bring to a boil and boil for five minutes. Add cranberries and cook five minutes longer until all the cranberries have popped and become transparent. Skim foam off carefully and discard. Mix in orange marmalade and lemon juice. Chill. Stir in almonds before serving.

HORSERADISH CREAM

½ cup heavy cream
2 tbsp. prepared horseradish
1 tbsp. lemon juice
¼ tsp. salt

Whip cream until stiff; add remaining ingredients slowly as you continue to beat. Serve chilled.

TOMATO SAUCE

1 (1 lb.) can (2 cups) tomatoes
1 onion, stuck with 3 cloves
1 cup chopped celery
½ cup chopped green pepper
1 carrot, diced
2 tbsp. chopped parsley
1 bay leaf
3 tbsp. butter
2 tbsp. flour
¼ tsp. sugar
1 tsp. basil

In a saucepan, combine tomatoes, onion, celery, green pepper, carrot, parsley and bay leaf. Bring to a boil, then simmer for 30 minutes. Strain (be sure to get all the pulpy residue). Melt butter; add flour and stir until blended. Add tomato mixture, sugar and basil. Simmer for 5 to 10 minutes.

PUMPKIN PARFAIT PIE

½ cup butter (1 stick) at room temperature
2 tbsp. sugar
1 cup flour
⅔ cup sugar
¼ cup water
1 egg white, unbeaten
½ tsp. cinnamon
1 tsp. lemon juice
½ tsp. nutmeg
½ tsp. ginger
1 cup heavy cream
¼ cup cooked pumpkin, well drained

Preheat oven to 375°. Combine butter and two tablespoons sugar until blended. Add flour; mix just until a dough forms. Reserve ¼ cup dough for topping; crumble dough. Press remaining dough evenly onto bottom and sides of 9-inch pie plate. Bake for 10 to 12 minutes. Cool.

Combine ⅔ cup sugar, water, egg white, cinnamon, lemon juice, nutmeg and ginger. Beat for 3 to 5 minutes or until soft peaks form. Beat heavy cream and pumpkin together until thick. Fold into egg white mixture gently. Spoon into baked crust. Sprinkle with reserved crumbs. Freeze until firm (about four to six hours).

Dessert Fondues

A dessert fondue—what a novel idea!

Oh, you've probably heard of—and maybe tried—chocolate fondue. But have you ever sampled a liqueur-flavored Grasshopper Fondue, a delicate fruit-flavored Melba Fondue, a Caramel Cream, or a candy-like and distinctively American Sugar on Snow? If these sound intriguing, read on—and do plan to try some (or all!) of our special dessert fondues.

Before you dip right in, though, heed these few guidelines. A dessert fondue should be served in a dish that can be kept warm at the table. Earthenware or ovenproof pottery are both good choices. A candle flame provides sufficient heat; too-high heat will scorch the fondue.

What are good dippers? Cubes of angel food, sponge or pound cake (toasted, if you like); chunks of doughnuts; ladyfingers; tiny cream puffs; orange or tangerine sections; strawberries; mandarin orange segments; thick banana slices; cherries; large marshmallows; peach slices; apple slices; fresh pear slices; pineapple chunks; tiny meringues.

For leisurely after-dinner service, have dessert in your living room, recreation room, or den. Put the fondue pot on a coffee table or right on the floor—in both cases on an asbestos mat, of course.

This may be the first time your guests have ever eaten dessert casually leaning against the pillows you have thoughtfully provided. But we'll guess it won't be the last time they'll want to.

Dessert fondue is a tasty way to end any meal—and, come to think of it, a tasty way to end this book.

CLASSIC CHOCOLATE FONDUE

3 (3 oz.) Toblerone candy bars
(Swiss chocolate bars)
½ cup cream

2 tbsp. kirsch, cognac or
Cointreau
Dippers of your choice

Melt the chocolate over hot water or very low flame. Stir in the cream and kirsch.

Note: This classic fondue may be varied by substituting crème de café for the kirsch, and adding one tablespoon instant coffee or ¼ teaspoon ground cloves and ¼ teaspoon cinnamon instead of liqueur.

WHITE CHOCOLATE FONDUE

3 (3 oz.) white chocolate
candy bars
½ cup cream

Jigger kirsch
Dippers of your choice

Heat white chocolate with cream. When melted, add kirsch.

Note: There is a white chocolate candy bar containing cocoa butter and crushed almonds which can be used in this recipe. Otherwise substitute good quality almond bark.

CHOCOLATE GLAZE

4 oz. unsweetened chocolate
4 oz. sweet cooking chocolate
½ cup butter (1 stick)

3 tbsp. honey
Dippers of your choice

Melt the chocolate over simmering water or very low flame. Stir in the butter and honey. Keep hot over low flame (use asbestos pad).

GRASSHOPPER FONDUE

12 oz. chocolate mint
"meltaways"
⅓ cup cream
Crème de menthe

Crème de cacao
Dippers of your choice

Melt the chocolate with cream. Add the liqueurs, one tablespoon at a time each, to taste. Add more cream if desired.

MAPLE RUM CHOCOLATE DELIGHT

1 pint very rich chocolate ice
   cream
½ cup pure maple syrup

Jigger rum
2 tsp. cornstarch or arrowroot
Dippers of your choice

Melt ice cream in the fondue pot with the maple syrup, stirring well. Mix rum with cornstarch. When ice cream has melted, add the rum mixture and stir well. Keep hot over a very low flame.

ORANGE CHOCOLATE

3 (3 oz.) orange-flavored
   chocolate bars
½ cup cream

Jigger Grand Marnier
Dippers of your choice

Melt chocolate with cream. Add liqueur.

RASPBERRY OR STRAWBERRY CREAM

3 (3 oz.) rich chocolate bars
½ cup cream

Jigger raspberry or strawberry
liqueur
Dippers of your choice

Melt chocolate with cream. Add liqueur.

CHOCOLATE ICE CREAM FONDUE

1 pint rich chocolate ice cream
Jigger kirsch or cognac

2 tsp. cornstarch or arrowroot
Dippers of your choice

Melt the ice cream; mix kirsch with cornstarch and stir in.

Note: This is less rich than fondue made with a candy bar, but just as delicious. If extra-rich chocolate ice cream is not available, use regular chocolate ice cream plus about ½ cup chocolate chips.

SAN FRANCISCO FUDGE

1 cup milk chocolate fudge
   topping

¼ cup California port
Dippers of your choice

Heat fudge topping in the fondue pot. When hot and thinned, stir in the port. Heat thoroughly.

DESSERT FONDUES

BLACKBERRY FONDUE

¾ cup water
½ cup sugar
2 cups blackberries

Juice of ½ lemon (2 tbsp.)
Jigger blackberry brandy
Dippers of your choice

Boil the water and sugar together for five minutes. Add the berries and cook until soft. Stir in the lemon juice and puree the fruit in a blender, then strain to remove seeds. (Or force through a strainer.) Add brandy. Serve hot or icy cold.

MELBA FONDUE

1 (10 oz.) pkg. frozen raspberries, thawed
1 (3 oz.) jar bar-le-duc (or red currant preserves with ¼ cup sugar)

1 tbsp. kirsch, framboise or water
1 tbsp. arrowroot or cornstarch
Dippers of your choice

Puree the raspberries and strain to remove seeds. Combine the puree with the bar-le-duc in the fondue pot; mix kirsch with arrowroot and stir in. Heat almost to boiling and keep hot over low flame.

Note: Guests can dunk the usual chunks of cake and pieces of fruit. Or buy heat-and-eat Italian bread and give guests small plates of bread chunks, unheated and unbrowned. The guests dunk the bread into the Melba Fondue, then into a bowl of whipped cream.

SUGAR ON SNOW

Butter the rim of a large saucepan. Pour into it ½ gallon pure maple syrup and bring to boil over low heat until syrup reaches 247°. Do not stir. Cool to 180°. Meanwhile fill pie plates with shaved ice—one plate for each guest. When the syrup is ready, bring it to the table and give each guest a wooden spoon. Guests drizzle the syrup over the ice from the spoons and twirl the resulting taffy onto forks to eat.

CARAMEL CREAM

1 (14 oz.) bag caramels	Banana slices
½ cup cream	Marshmallows
1 oz. kirsch	Chopped nuts

Melt caramels with cream over low heat or in top of a double boiler. Stir occasionally until sauce is smooth. Stir in kirsch. Spear fruit on marshmallows; dip in caramel cream. Roll in chopped nuts.

MIDSUMMER ICE

1 (10 oz.) pkg. frozen raspberries, thawed	Peaches
Sugar and kirsch to taste	Meringues
Whipped cream	Ice cream

Rub fruit through a sieve to remove seeds. Flavor with sugar and kirsch and pour into a glass bowl. Chill well—an hour or so in the freezer will do. Set the bowl in a larger bowl of shaved ice and bring to the table. Guests each have a bowl of whipped cream sweetened with a little sugar and vanilla. They dip fresh peaches, meringues and small ice cream balls into the sauce, then the whipped cream.

CHOCOLATE FONDUE

1 (6 oz.) pkg. semisweet chocolate chips	2 tbsp. brandy or rum (optional)
½ cup light corn syrup	Dash cinnamon
1 tsp. vanilla or 1½ tsp. instant coffee powder	Dippers of your choice

Combine chocolate chips and corn syrup over hot (not boiling) water; stir until chocolate melts and is smooth. Add remaining ingredients; stir until well blended. Keep warm.

Note: You can substitute two tablespoons orange juice for the brandy and omit cinnamon, if you prefer.

Index

Index

Index